Kathy Lamancusa's

Guide to

Floral Design

TAB TAB BOOKS
Blue Ridge Summit, PA

Notices

Sahara II®   Smithers—Oasis Co.
Styrofoam®   Dow Chemical Corp.
Design Master®   Colorado Dye and Chemical Corp.
X-ACTO®   Hunt-Bienfang.

FIRST EDITION
FIRST PRINTING

Library of Congress Cataloging-in-Publication Data

Lamancusa, Kathy.
    [Guide to floral design]
    Kathy Lamancusa's guide to floral design / by Kathy Lamancusa.
        p.   cm.
    Includes index.
    ISBN 0-8306-7491-8   ISBN 0-8306-3491-6 (pbk.)
    1. Flower arrangement.   I. Title: Floral design.
    SB449.L28   1990   90-37848
    745.92—dc20   CIP

TAB BOOKS offers software for sale. For information and a catalog, please
contact TAB Software Department, Blue Ridge Summit, PA 17294-0850.

Questions regarding the content of this book should be addressed to:

    Reader Inquiry Branch
    TAB BOOKS
    Blue Ridge Summit, PA 17294-0850

Acquisitions Editor: Kim Tabor
Edited and Designed by Joanne Slike
Production: Katherine G. Brown
Page Makeup: Kimberly Shockey
Cover Design: Lori E. Schlosser

Full page and cover photography by
Shawn Wood, Studio 7, North Canton, OH

Contents

ꙮAcknowledgmentsꙮ

I would like to thank the following people who assisted in making this book a reality:

Joe—my husband who was supportive every step of the way and who handled the technical aspects of the book

Katherine Lamancusa—my sister-in-law who helped design some of the projects in this book

Mary Annette Salpietra—my friend who assisted with some of the step-by-step photos as well as the instruction writing

Joey and *Jimmy*—my sons who constantly asked me how the book was going and accepted thrown together meals and late laundry during its preparation

S. Joseph Lamancusa—my father-in-law who made the wood carvings shown in the masculine color photo, on page 7 of the color section

Josephine Lamancusa—my mother-in-law who made the painted ducks in the same photo

ꙮSuppliersꙮ

The following companies supplied product for use in the preparation of this book:

AMERICAN OAK PRESERVING CO.
601 Mulberry St.
North Judson, IN 46366

B.B. WORLD CORP.
2200 So. Maple Avenue
Los Angeles, CA 90011

CUSTOMFOAM CRAFTS
1 Longfellow Place
Ludington, MI 49431

C.M. OFFRAY & SON INC.
Route 24 Box 601
Chester, N.J. 07903

DESIGN MASTER COLOR TOOL INC.
P.O. Box 601
Boulder, CO 80306

LION RIBBON COMPANY
100 Metro Way
Secaucus, N.J. 07096

LOCTITE CORP.
4450 Cranwood Court
Cleveland, OH 44128

LOMEY MANUFACTURING CORP.
P.O. Box 5314
Asheville, N.C. 28813

MALGO CRAFTS
302 West 1st Street
Montrose, MO 64770

RHYNE FLORAL SUPPLY
P.O. Box 310
Gastonia, N.C. 28053

SMITHERS—OASIS CO.
919 Marvin Avenue
Kent, OH 44240

ZUCKER FEATHER PRODUCTS
512 North East Street
California, MO 65018

Introduction

*I*t is not necessary to create a large, elaborate arrangement or use exotic materials to achieve fulfillment in floral design. A child's bouquet of flowers brought to mom is just as beautiful as any large arrangement; flowers picked from the garden and placed in a simple container are as enjoyable as any exotic design. The sincerity involved in creating the design is what makes each arrangement special.

Yet learning a few basics about floral design will allow you to confidently create more and more elaborate designs—and virtually anyone can master these basic techniques. Beginning floral students will learn to express themselves creatively through flowers; more advanced students will value this guide as a wealth of floral ideas to use as stepping-off points. Once you are thoroughly familiar with the elements that make up a successful design, you will be able to "break the rules," incorporating some of your own ideas, and still have a balanced, harmonious arrangement.

Kathy Lamancusa's Guide to Floral Design contains everything you will need to know as you begin a journey into the beautiful world of flower arranging. As I developed the contents, I remembered back to when I was a beginning flower arranging student, then I tried to answer all the questions I had at that time.

Part One begins with lists and descriptions of the basic tools and materials vital to floral design. It then describes the various flowers you will need to purchase and the principles and design elements essential to successful floral design. You won't be sent off hunting for rare or exotic materials, either; all are available at any number of craft stores or flower shops. (Although this book deals only with silk and dried materials, you can create all of the designs with fresh flowers using the same floral steps. However, be sure to use Oasis® floral arranging foam instead of Sahara® Only Oasis is intended to hold water necessary for fresh flowers.)

Part Two covers the various kinds of designs. Each chapter begins with general instructions, followed by specific design projects that tie into the main lesson in that chapter. The checklists included throughout are a unique feature: they discuss areas that could potentially go wrong as you create the design. Knowing about these pitfalls beforehand makes each design virtually foolproof.

Part Three contains over 30 projects, ranging from simple country-style designs to elegant Victorian designs. With each project you are given complete materials lists and step-by-step instructions, along with a photo showing the finished piece. Many of the designs are ideal for gift-giving; they are easy to make and perfect for that last-minute gift idea. Included are everyday designs, and designs for special occasions and holidays.

Enjoy flower arranging. Let it bring you hours of pleasure

Starting Out

Success in floral design depends on having the proper supplies and materials and knowing how to use them. When first beginning flower arranging, you must make a certain investment in tools and materials. You can find all of the supplies mentioned in this book at any well-stocked floral or craft store.

TOOLS & SUPPLIES

A great deal of time and effort can be saved by simply having the right supplies. Let's discuss each of the tools and supplies that are important.

☐ *Scissors and wire cutters* (FIG. 1-1). A good set of wire cutters is extremely important. Invest in a pair that is top quality and they will last a long time. These cutters are used to cut any materials that are wire or have wire cores.

Two different sizes of scissors are shown. Choose the size that is comfortable for your hand. These scissors are used to cut ribbons and

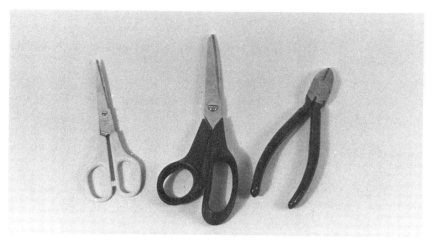

Fig. 1-1
Good-quality scissors and wire cutters are valuable design tools.

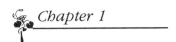

other non-wire items. Never attempt to cut wire with your good scissors; the blades will get nicked and scratched, and in a short time, will no longer cut ribbon.

☐ *Serrated knife.* A serrated knife is used to cut floral foams to achieve a smooth, even cut.

☐ *Ruler or tape measure.* The ruler or tape measure is used to accurately determine the width and height of the arrangement, as well as assisting in determining proper flower stem length.

☐ *Floral tape.* Floral tape is a non-sticky tape available in green, white, brown, and other colors. It is used in a multitude of ways in floral design.

☐ *Hot-glue guns and glue sticks* (FIG. 1-2). Glue guns are indispensable to floral designers. When proper care is taken, they are fast and easy to use and offer superior bonding on a number of surfaces.

Fig. 1-2
Hot-glue guns and glue sticks create a superior bond for many floral needs.

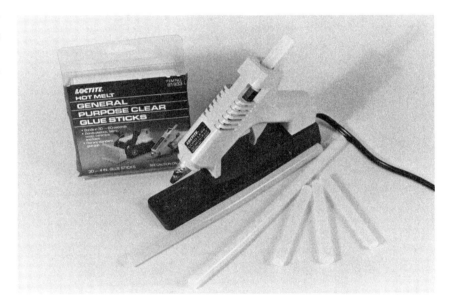

Glue guns use shaped glue sticks, which are a mixture of plastics, resins, and adhesives. They are inserted into the back of the gun and pass through a heating chamber that melts and activates the glue. The glue gun extrudes quantities of glue that have been melted to a temperature of 350°F. Because of the temperature of the glue, this product should be kept away from children.

Hot-melt adhesives form a secure bond within 30 to 90 seconds following application. Most hot-melt adhesives will be affected by temperature and weather changes and caution should be taken when using them outdoors.

☐ *Pins* (FIG. 1-3). The U-shaped pins on the left of the photo have several different names: pole pins, greening pins, craft pins, U-pins, and so on. They are used to attach moss onto foam and to attach materials to wreaths or table floral designs.

　　The corsage pins pictured in the center are used to attach ribbons or other similar materials to foams or wreaths. Because of their large, decorative pin heads, they are used when they will be seen for decorative purposes.

　　Straight pins, pictured on the right side of the photo, are invaluable items with hundreds of uses. They are available in many pin lengths as well as with various sizes of pin heads. Decide what is best for you by the materials you will be working with.

☐ *Stem wire* (FIG. 1-4). Wire is available in natural color as well as green-painted. It is also available in a number of diameters or gauges. The smaller the gauge of number identified, the thinner the wire will be. For example, 30-gauge (ga.) wire is much thinner than 16-gauge (ga.) wire.

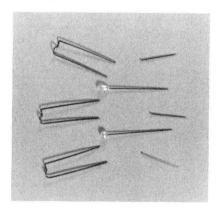

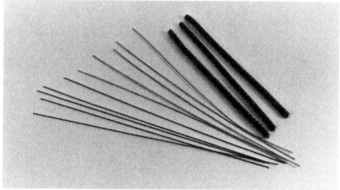

Green-painted wire is usually more costly and most often will end up being floral-taped, so there is no great need to purchase green over natural. Usually used to lengthen flower stems, 20-gauge wire will also help support softer drieds or flowers.

　　The chenille stems shown in the right portion of the photo are useful for securing bows and can be inserted into foams. These stems are wires twisted with tiny chenille fibers. When you are attaching two pieces of foam together, chenille stems are ideal to use; the fibers do not allow the stems to pull away from the foam as a bare wire would do.

Fig. 1-3 (Left)
Pole pins, corsage pins, and straight pins are necessary items to add to your floral tool collection.

Fig. 1-4 (Right)
Stem wire and chenille stems assist in many applications.

☐ *Wooden pick* (FIG. 1-5). A wooden pick has one blunt end and one pointed end. A wire is attached to the blunt end and is used to wrap around items secured to the pick. The pointed end is used to insert

Fig. 1-5
Wood picks are useful when lengthening stems, clustering dried materials, and forming ribbon loops.

materials into the design. In the photo you will see three ways wooden picks are used for floral design: forming ribbon loops, creating a firm stem for a cluster of dried materials, and lengthening silk flower stems.

To attach a wood pick, lay the wired end of the pick against the item, overlapping at least ½ inch (1.27 cm). Wrap the wire securely around the item and pick a few times, then down around the stems only a few times, and then back up and around the item and wood pick again. This will help eliminate twisting and turning on the wood pick.

☐ *Tape adhesive.* This tape is a very sticky, putty-like tape for attaching Styrofoam® into containers. It can also be used to attach other items to floral containers whenever using hot glue is inappropriate.

FOAMS & MOSSES

Foam and moss are two vital items in the construction of floral designs. When creating a design, you insert flowers and materials into the foam. Then you use the moss to cover the foam so that it is not noticed in the finished design.

Foam Types and Techniques

Your choice of foam is very important to your finished floral design. Each type of arranging foam is designed to suit a particular need. Because of the various compositions of each foam, each type must be attached to its container in a different manner. Refer to FIG. 1-6 for types of foams.

Fig. 1-6
Each floral foam product fits a specific need.

☐ *Silk and dried foam* (Sahara®) (back left of photo). This material is used for any type of dried or silk materials you wish to incorporate into the design. It is a softer foam, so you need not reinforce dried stems with wire before inserting them into the foam.

Dried floral foam is a bit sandier in consistency than plastic foams; therefore, it will not stick with the use of tape adhesive. To cut the foam, simply use a serrated knife.

To attach, first cut the foam to fit the shape of the container, allowing some space surrounding the foam, and glue into the container using hot glue or tacky glue (FIG. 1-7). The foam can also be attached by inserting U-shaped pieces of chenille up through the bottom of the basket and into the foam in three equally spaced locations.

If the bottom of the basket is extremely uneven, another method is to place the foam into the container, cover it with moss, and then insert the end of a piece of thin wire through the wicker on the basket and twist the ends (FIG. 1-8). Repeat on the opposite side of the basket,

Fig. 1-7 (Below Left)
Hot glue is the best method of attaching foam to a container.

Fig. 1-8 (Below Right)
One method of attaching foam to a basket is to wrap one end of a length of cloth-covered wire around the basket edge and twist.

directly across from the first location. Bring the two wires together and twist them in the center to secure. Trim away all but approximately 1 inch (2.54 cm) wire on each length. Then bend this extra wire under and insert into the foam (FIG. 1-9). Repeat this process with two wires in the opposite direction so that there are four equally spaced wires on the basket.

Fig. 1-9
After attaching a wire on the opposite side, twist both ends in the center of the foam.

For ease of construction, Sahara is also available in "caged form" such as the Lomey large caged foam shown in the front center of FIG. 1-6. These pieces are simply glued into the container or used as a base itself for the arranging of flowers.

☐ *Plastic foam* (Styrofoam). Plastic foam is a firmer foam that can be used for either silk or dried materials. It is available in many different sizes and shapes in green or white, as shown on the right side of FIG. 1-6. The thinner stems of dried materials will need to be reinforced with a wood pick or floral-taped to a piece of stem wire to insert easily into this foam.

To attach plastic foam to the container use three small balls of tape adhesive placed on the bottom of the foam. Press the foam down and twist to spread the tape adhesive and create a stronger bond.

The plastic foam may also be attached with glue or, if using a basket, U-shaped pieces of chenille stems can be inserted through the bottom of the basket and into the foam in three places equally spaced around.

☐ *Wet foam* (Oasis®). This foam is used for *fresh flowers only*! Do not attempt to use it for silk arrangements because it is very soft and will fall apart over a period of time, after the arrangement is made. Any of the designs shown in this book can also be completed with fresh flowers. Simply follow the same directions, replacing the dried foam with a wet foam.

To use, soak the wet foam in water for 5 to 10 minutes until the block sinks to the water level. Cut it with a knife to the shape of the container. It can be attached by using Oasis glue or spreading Oasis tape over the top of the foam and down the sides of the container.

Container preparation.

Follow these tips for all three kinds of foam explained above:

○ The foam should extend above the top of the container approximately 1 inch (2.54 cm) or two fingers, as shown in FIG. 1-10.

○ Leave at least ½ inch (1.27 cm) to 1 inch (2.54 cm) on all sides of foam so moss can be tucked around it (FIG. 1-11).

○ For wet foams, cut a wedge on one side so the arrangement can be watered daily.

○ If foam is not tall enough to extend ½ (1.27 cm) to 1 inch (2.54 cm) over the top of the container, cut three 2-inch (5.08 cm) pieces of chenille stem and insert them equally spaced in the bottom piece, which is secured to the container. Cut a second piece of foam to fit on top of the first piece and extend above the container. Place this piece on top of the first piece, inserting it into the chenille stems to secure both together. Do not use glue to attach the two pieces together: if you must temporarily leave the arrangement and the glue has had a chance to dry before completion of the arrangement, it will be difficult to insert the stems.

Fig. 1-10 (Above Left) Foam should extend above the basket edge two fingers high.

Fig. 1-11 (Above Right) Cut foam so that it fits inside the basket but so that some space remains between the foam and the container for moss.

Floral Mosses

Moss is used to cover your foam so that it does not show. Never eliminate the moss. You rarely notice the moss in a well-constructed arrangement, but you will surely notice a bare piece of foam through the flowers in a design. Various types of moss are available. Choose one that will best accent the design you are creating (FIG. 1-12).

☐ *Spanish moss* (shown at the left side in FIG. 1-12). This moss is a greyish color and is used more for natural-looking arrangements. It is also available in green-dyed; however, this color tends to be too bright a green and stands out in the design.

☐ *Excelsior* (shown in the center back of FIG. 1-12). Excelsior is a form of shredded wood shavings. Bleached excelsior is the most popular, although other colors are available. Excelsior is mostly used for country or kitchen designs, but can also can be added for a unique color and texture change.

☐ *Natural moss* (shown in the center front of FIG. 1-12). This material, found in the woods, is then peeled away, fumigated, and used for floral designs. It is available in natural, which has a brownish-green look to it, or dyed. Like dyed Spanish moss, dyed natural moss tends to be too bright. Because it is more noticeable in the finished piece, it may detract from the overall design.

☐ *Shredded iridescent plastic* (shown on the right of FIG. 1-12). This material, formed from iridescent plastic sheets, is most often used for Easter or high-style designs.

Fig. 1-12 (Below Left) Many types of mosses are available on the market.

Fig. 1-13 (Below Right) Secure moss to foam with a "U" shaped craft pin.

To attach any of the above mosses, simply spread them over the top of the foam and down around the sides. A complete, but thin coat is best. Insert a few pole pins through the moss and into the foam to secure (FIG. 1-13). Never glue the moss to the foam as it will then be too difficult to insert flower stems into the foam through the glued moss.

FLORAL CONTAINERS

There is no limit to the types, styles, or colors of containers you may wish to use. Follow the guidelines given for each type of arrangement you choose to make, but remember, you can use your imagination and create any of the styles of designs described in this book in any type of container that fits the general container requirements of that design. A container can be anything from a fine piece of crystal to an old shoe. Make your arrangements and containers complement each other in terms of the florals and drieds used. Figures 1-14 to 1-17 show many different types of containers available.

Fig. 1-14 (Top Left) Unusual containers such as mugs, muslin sacks, and egg baskets make unique arrangements.

Fig. 1-15 (Top Right) Low containers are perfect for many arrangement styles.

Fig. 1-16 Old-fashioned country looks can be achieved with the use of various wicker or wooden containers.

Fig. 1-17 Round containers, either with or without handles, are nice for round designs.

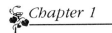

FLORAL TAPING

Floral tape is not a sticky tape. It is actually a waxed crepe-paper material that only sticks to itself when stretched. Available in white, green, black, brown, as well as other pastel colors, floral tape color should coordinate with the colors used in the design. Choose pastel colors only when green or brown are inappropriate. Floral tape is useful when lengthening flower stems or attaching materials such as clusters of dried flowers to lengths of wire for insertion into floral designs (FIG. 1-18).

Fig. 1-18
Floral tape in white or green is useful to lengthen stems or reinforce thin-stemmed dried materials to wire.

To use:
1. Hold the item or stems to be floral-taped in your left hand. Hold the roll of floral tape in your right hand, with the tape between your thumb and forefinger and the roll of tape resting on your little finger. Wrap the end of the floral tape around the top of the stem and squeeze so the end adheres to the tape and holds the stem.
2. Begin to twist the stem with your left hand, holding the tape firmly and stretching it slightly. (The stretching helps to activate the adhesive abilities.) Continue to turn the stem, stretching and angling the tape downward as you go. Floral-tape all the way to the end of the stem, breaking and squeezing the tape at the end (FIG. 1-19).

When lengthening or reinforcing stems, use 20-gauge wire at the necessary length. Lay the wire next to the item to be taped, so that the wire extends at least 1 inch (2.54 cm) beyond the end of the item. If the original flower stem is 3 inches (7.62 cm) or less, lay the wire next to the flower stem all the way up to the calyx (base) of the flower. Floral-tape the entire length of both stems together.

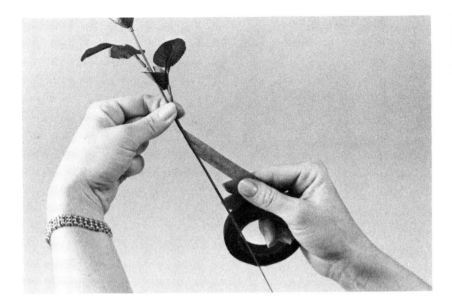

Fig. 1-19
Hold the stem in your
left hand and floral tape in
your right.

ARRANGEMENT STABILITY

To make flower stems insert easily into the foam, first cut the stems at an angle with the wire cutters. Then dip the ends into tacky glue before inserting into the foam so that they do not twist or turn in the finished design.

Some silk flower heads tend to fall off their stems. To eliminate this, remove the flower head from the stem, dip it into tacky glue, and replace it on the stem.

Flowers & Ribbons

*K*nowing floral terminology and definitions is important when creating flower arrangements so that you will know what to ask for when purchasing supplies, and so that you can confidently choose the most appropriate flower types for the design you wish to create. In addition, knowing how to incorporate ribbons and bows will add a special touch to almost any design. Keep in mind, however, that mastering techniques used in making bows does require a bit of practice—but the results will be well worth your efforts.

FLOWER TYPES

Flower types are broken down into three categories, which constitute the entire range of flowers used in design: *line flowers*, *mass flowers*, and *filler flowers*.

Line flowers are long, thin, tapering materials that are always used at the extremities or outer portions of the design. The purpose of the line flower is to bring your eye to the center or heart of the design. Figure 2-1 shows three examples of line flowers: freesia, eucalyptus, and pussy willow.

Usually the primary flowers used in a design, *mass flowers* are round, many-petalled flowers. These flowers are useful for filling space in the design as well as acting as the main feature of the arrangement. Figure 2-2 shows a few examples of mass flowers: a rose, daffodil, and carnation.

Filler flowers are smaller flowers with many heads on one stem. The varieties of the type are endless. The purpose of filler flowers is to add variation of color or texture, or to fill space in the design. Fillers need not be confined to flowers; materials such as ribbon bows or loops are also considered "fillers." Figure 2-3 shows three types of filler flowers.

There are many types of dried flower fillers on the market today, though most of the filler materials are really preserved and not dried. Preserving makes materials more supple, easier to handle, and not as brittle.

Fig. 2-1 (Above Left)
Line flowers are long, thin, and tapering.

Fig. 2-2 (Above Right)
Mass flowers are usually the main flowers in the design.

Fig. 2-3 (Left)
Filler materials are available in many varieties.

Sprigs of flowers are the small groupings on each stem that contain three to four flower heads. Try to cut the sprigs away from the main stem at a joint, retaining some of the main stem wire. This eliminates the need to tape them to a wire for insertion.

PURCHASING & MEASURING FLOWERS

The material lists for the projects contained in this book list the exact type and style of flower used in the design. You may have trouble finding these materials in their exact configurations. This will happen more often with silk flowers, since many styles are sold in the market. Therefore, when purchasing flowers, be sure to buy the number of flowers you need, instead of the number of stems listed. For example, suppose the directions say: ''Two stems roses with two open flowers and two buds per stem,'' but your store only has rose stems containing one open flower and one rosebud. In this case, instead of buying two stems as specified, you would need to purchase four stems to get the correct number of flowers.

Figure 2-4 shows one stem of flowers that would be described as: ''One stem of lilies with two groups, each containing three 2-inch (5 cm) open lilies and one bud.'' Figure 2-5 shows a stem of silk double blossoms that would be described as: ''One stem of double silk blossoms with six sprigs.''

Figure 2-6 shows a stem of eucalyptus that would be described as: ''One eucalyptus stem with a 12-inch (30.5 cm) leaf portion.'' This means that you need measure the leaf portion only; the stem is not included in this measurement. When the instructions call for a 14-inch (35 cm) eucalyptus stem, you would measure the entire stem from the tip all the way down to the end of the stem.

Fig. 2-4 (Below Left) This lily stem has two groups of flowers.

Fig. 2-5 (Below Middle) This filler has six sprigs.

Fig. 2-6 (Below Right) Measure the leaf portion of a eucalyptus stem from the tip to the end of the leaf portion.

Top

End of leaf portion

When measuring flower stems to cut, lay the flower in its proper location, resting on the foam, mark where the stem will meet the foam, and add 1 inch (2.5 cm) to 2 inches (5 cm), depending on the size of the foam. Then cut at this spot.

RIBBON TECHNIQUES

Ribbon can add a wonderful accent to any design, whether you use a bow or only a few ribbon loops.

To form a ribbon loop:

1. Cut a piece of ribbon the length indicated, bring the ends together, and lay a wood pick next to the ends of the ribbon.
2. Wrap the wire snugly around the ribbon ends and the wood pick.
3. For a single streamer of ribbon, simply attach a wood pick to the end of a piece of ribbon (FIG. 2-7).

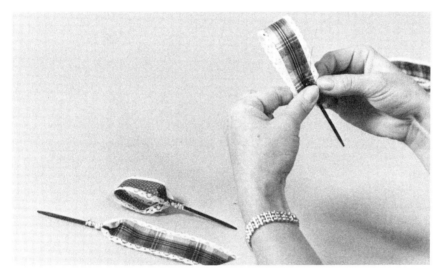

Fig. 2-7
Ribbon loops make perfect filler materials.

To form a ribbon bow:

1. Begin by forming a loop of ribbon the size necessary and holding it between the thumb and forefinger of your left hand (FIG. 2-8).
2. If you are using a ribbon that has a right and wrong side, twist the bottom portion of the ribbon so that you again see the right side (FIG. 2-9).
3. Form a second loop with the lower portion of ribbon, bringing it to the back and then again pinching between your thumb and forefinger (FIG. 2-10).
4. Again, twist the ribbon to see the right side and form a third loop.
5. Continue in this fashion during the construction of one more loop.

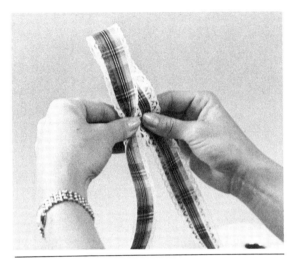

Fig. 2-8 (Above)
The first step for making a bow is to form the first loop.

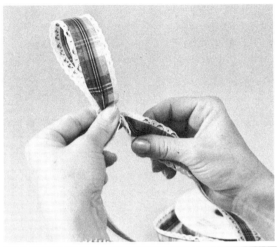

Fig. 2-9 (Above)
Twist the ribbon when it has a right and wrong side.

Fig. 2-10 (Above Left)
Form the second loop below the first loop.

Fig. 2-11 (Above Right)
The center loop is formed when you are halfway done with the bow.

6. After you have one-half the loops you will be making, add the loop in the center. To do this, simply form a small loop of ribbon around your thumb as shown in FIG. 2-11 and pinch the back portion of ribbon again between your thumb and forefinger.

7. Continue adding at least four loops, or more if desired, in the same manner as described above.

8. When finished, insert a cloth-covered wire or chenille stem through the center loop. Bring the ends to the back and twist securely.

ENHANCING FLOWER COLORS

Many colors of flowers are available on the market today, but sometimes it is difficult to find just the right one to suit our needs. When this happens, the use of a color tool will give you the exact color you need. Do not use a spray paint, as this will make the petals of your flowers very stiff. Instead, use Design Master® spray, which is more like a floral dye than a paint. It will leave your flower petals soft to the touch, yet allow you the versatility of color that its complete assortment encourages. To use, hold the can away from the flowers and mist the petals with color. Build up the color in steps, rather than spraying until the deepest color is achieved. You will be much happier with the results (FIG. 2-12).

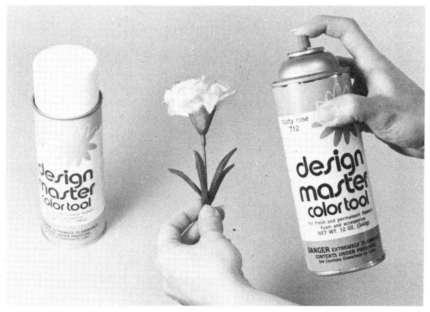

Fig. 2-12
Design Master sprays are the perfect tool for floral color enhancement.

The Basics of Design

*W*hen creating a floral design, there are two aspects you should be concerned with: the technical and the visual. The technical aspect includes such elements as stability, point of origin, and balance—in other words the "engineering" of the design. Such elements are not outwardly evident, but they are important to the overall results. The visual aspect encompasses design elements and principles used to make the design aesthetically appealing, such as form, space, line, texture, unity, scale, accent, and color. These are the elements that we notice and respond to, whether consciously or subconsciously.

THE TECHNICAL ASPECT

The technical aspect also encompasses what is termed the *mechanics* of the design. Mechanics refer to the materials vital to the creation of the arrangement, for example, floral foams, adhesives, wires, and floral tape. In a properly created design, the mechanics will become invisible.

Now, let's look more closely at the elements that make up the technical aspect.

Stability

Stability is crucial to the success of any floral design. The floral container must be prepared as explained in chapter 1 so that the design remains firm even through transit. Any accessories or accent objects and materials must also be attached firmly to the base or container. The means of attaching each object or material will vary depending on the item used.

Point of Origin

The point of origin refers to the place where all stems appear to meet. Although all stems cannot be inserted into the foam at the identical location, in most designs, they should seem to be connected in one spot located near the center of the foam. The center flower should be vertical in the design. All others should angle into the foam, with those resting on the container edge parallel to the table. Of vital importance to the overall visual aspects of the design, the point of origin should be constantly checked as the design is created. Figure 3-1 shows an arrangement with the proper point of origin; FIG. 3-2 shows an improper one.

Balance

The balance of a design is controlled by the placement of the floral materials in the container. When making the various designs explained in this book, pay particularly close attention to the instructions describing where each stem should be inserted. The overall look of a round design style should be uniformly round. Strict attention should be paid to the midpoint lines of curved designs. If the flowers are placed beyond the line, the design will appear unbalanced. Most of the stems of a line design should be inserted into the back half of the foam. Too many stems placed in front of the foam will make the design look like it is falling forward. You have balanced the design correctly if it looks sturdy enough to stand on its own and does not appear to be toppling over.

Fig. 3-1 (Above Left)
This floral arrangement shows the proper point of origin.

Fig. 3-2 (Above Right)
This floral design shows an improper point of origin.

THE VISUAL ASPECTS

The first question you should ask yourself when making a floral arrangement is: "What shape will the design be?". *Form* is the overall shape of the arrangement. It includes the height, width, and depth of the design. Chapter 4 will explain in detail round designs forms, chapter 5 deals with the forms of curve designs, and chapter 6 describes the proper formation of line designs forms.

Space

The use of space is a vital consideration when planning any floral design. The goal is not necessarily to completely fill space, only to present the composition by using the space as effectively as possible.

Every element and item used to fill space interacts with the space it occupies. The two work as a team. There are three ways materials can occupy space in a design.

1. *Positive space* is the space filled by items or flowers.
2. *Negative space* is space that is totally empty. This includes the space surrounding items and flowers.
3. *Voids* are spaces that connect. An example is the clean stem of a flower, which connects the blossom to the design. The voids left between elements are at times just as important as the materials themselves.

Negative space is used to enhance each element within the display and draw attention to the individual loveliness of different elements and groupings within the design. It gives special importance to the parts that make up the whole picture and allows the viewer to enjoy them.

Placing an emphasis on the positive space in a design creates a strong visual feeling of mass and abundance. Designs with emphasis placed on negative space will appear more contemporary and upscale.

Line

Properly created *line* in a design controls eye movement and establishes rhythm. Line will lead the viewer's eye along a definite path from one point to another. Keeping the lines used within our arrangement as simple as possible will allow them to demand attention. There are five primary types of lines that are used in floral design: vertical, horizontal, diagonal, curved, and circular.

Texture

Every item in our world possesses a texture. That texture is both visual as well as tactile. *Visual texture* is the result of light refracted from any surface. For example, a somewhat smooth surface will appear bright and shiny, such as a glass ball on a Christmas tree shining and glistening from the tree lights. A plastic or vinyl piece of fabric will appear wet when light touches it and rough or course surface will appear dull. Burlap sacks, straw bales, canvas or corduroy fabrics are all examples of materials that appear dull to our eyes.

Not only do we see texture through light reflection, we feel texture. *Tactile texture* can be rough or smooth, thick or thin, soft or hard, and course or fine.

Blending and combining textures creates a particular feeling in a design. Textures should be chosen for their contrast; however, to create the best effect, materials should be similar in the moods or feeling they evoke. No design should consist of identical textures in all elements as this is monotonous and not visually appealing.

When choosing materials for a design, think about the feeling or mood you wish the viewer to create in their minds. The feeling of romance can be achieved by combing the elegance of satin and moiré ribbons with the contrasting look of rich laces and baby's breath. As you will note although, we are combining similar ''romantic'' materials, they are of contrasting textures. The satins and moirés are smooth and shiny, while the laces and baby's breath are rough and dull.

If a country look is desired, why not combine materials that are similar in their rough look, such as burlap fabrics, wheat? Contrast these with the smooth look of pumpkins and apples and you will have a spectacular, interesting design that will excite the eye of your viewer and stimulate their minds to create a particular picture or feeling.

Unity

When all aspects of a design are successfully integrated, unity is achieved. Combining all elements in various textures, colors, and containers can be extremely challenging.

In beginning the thought processes to create a design, keep in mind that the whole design should carry a oneness of purpose, thought, and style. All the elements and accessories used should work toward a proper visual relationship. As in a musical score where all parts work together to form one beautiful sound, all items in the design should work together harmoniously.

Harmony in style and suitability for the occasion is vitally important. We must recognize the class distinctions between flowers and other accessories so that we can choose accordingly. For example, roses, satin, lace, and pearls are used to evoke a feeling of elegance; daisies, geraniums, carnations, gingham ribbon, and dried gypsophila are used for a more casual styling.

Repetition, or the repeating of color, texture, and shape throughout a design, is an essential element in achieving rhythm. For example, if a blue container is used for a design and yet no blue was incorporated anywhere else in the design, the piece would not look quite right. To unify and establish rhythm and harmony of the elements, some blue flowers, even if they be only tiny ones, must be added into the main part of the design. You could also use blue ribbon tufts or even an accessory piece such as a doll or stuffed animal that also contains some blue, in place of flowers.

Another important consideration for unity is that the design be appropriate to its surroundings and for the occasion created. Casual, non-fussy designs are best used in rooms of an informal nature and elegant pieces look more at home in more formal surroundings.

When creating seasonal or occasion pieces, think about what the viewer would expect to see, then plan from there. Changes and adaptations can be made. For a traditional Christmas styling, begin with pine, pine cones, and red velvet ribbon. For an elegant look, add metallic horns, candles, white doves, or poinsettias. If a whimsical look is the choice, add teddy bears, blocks, and other cute and cheerful elements.

The goal of unity is achieved only if several other principles of design have been well carried out. When last looking at the finished piece, you will know that you were successful if you have the personal feeling that everything goes together comfortably.

Scale

Each element in the design must be in a proper size relationship to all other elements in that design for the finished work to be in scale. A long-stemmed rose inserted into a 4-inch (10 cm) bud vase or three daisies placed into a 10-inch-wide (22.5 cm) basket are both examples of poor scale.

Accent

The *focal point* is the center of attention in a design. It can also be the point from which a design originates. Placing an unusual flower at the focal point creates an *accent*—for example, one single, special orchid placed in the center of the arrangement. Special items such as bows, dolls, toys, or heirloom pieces can also be added to accent the design.

Color

Color is a dynamic, radiant force of energy that breathes life into a design. Color will affect us positively or negatively by creating a mood or feeling. It puts emphasis where the designer wants it and gives visual balance to a design.

If you are creating a design whereby you rely on man-made items, such as silk florals and ribbons, you will need to adapt as best you can in matching colors and color schemes, since you will be relying on color created by others and not yourself. When using fresh floral materials, you must rely on the colors Mother Nature creates. These colors rarely match those on the color wheel exactly.

Color is an exciting challenge and knowing how to use it is crucial to the success of your designs. Let's learn some of the basics.

○ *Hue*—The hue of a color refers to the colors' name.

○ *Intensity*—The intensity of the color refers to the degree of color saturation.

○ *Value*—The value of a color refers to its lightness or darkness. It is affected by tints, shades, and tones. We'll use the color blue as we discuss these concepts below.

～ Tint: Mixing white with a hue produces a tint of that color. The tint of blue that results is baby blue.

～ Shade: Mixing black with a hue produces a shade of that color. The shade of blue that result is navy.

～ Tone: Mixing grey with a hue produces a tone of that color. The tone of blue that result is French blue. Often the Williamsburg colors, in their greyed-down states, are tones of their original colors.

THE COLOR WHEEL

A traditional color wheel consists of twelve hues of pure color at full strength. All the colors originate from the three *primary colors*: red, yellow, and blue. These primary colors must be found in their pure form. Nothing can be mixed to create them. Figure 3-3 shows the primary colors on the color wheel.

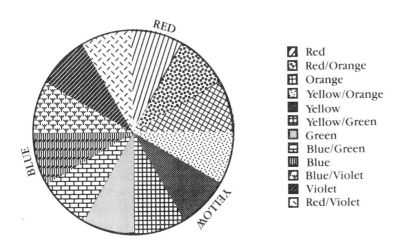

Fig. 3-3
The primary colors are easily identified on the color wheel.

☑ Red
☒ Red/Orange
⊞ Orange
☒ Yellow/Orange
■ Yellow
⊞ Yellow/Green
▦ Green
⊟ Blue/Green
▥ Blue
☒ Blue/Violet
▨ Violet
☒ Red/Violet

Secondary colors are created when two primary colors side-by-side on the color wheel are mixed in equal amounts:

Red and yellow = orange
Yellow and blue = green
Blue and red = violet

The secondary colors are orange, green, and violet. Figure 3-4 shows the secondary colors on the color wheel.

Intermediate colors, (sometimes called "tertiary" colors) are created when equal amounts of a primary and secondary color located side-by-side on the color wheel are mixed.

The intermediate colors are yellow-orange, yellow-green, blue-green, blue-violet, red-violet, and red-orange. Figure 3-5 shows the intermediate colors on the color wheel.

Fig. 3-4
The secondary colors are a combination of two primary colors on the color wheel.

Color Wheel

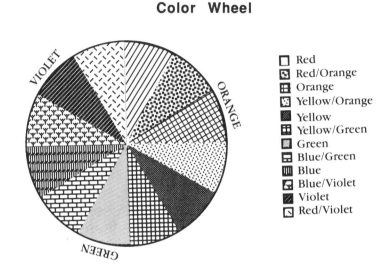

- ☐ Red
- ▨ Red/Orange
- ⊞ Orange
- ▦ Yellow/Orange
- ■ Yellow
- ⊞ Yellow/Green
- ▨ Green
- ⊟ Blue/Green
- ▥ Blue
- ▨ Blue/Violet
- ▦ Violet
- ◩ Red/Violet

Fig. 3-5
Intermediate colors are a combination of one primary and one secondary color.

Color Wheel

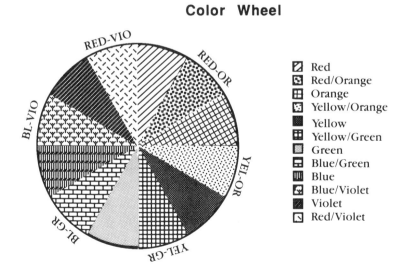

- ▨ Red
- ▨ Red/Orange
- ⊞ Orange
- ▦ Yellow/Orange
- ■ Yellow
- ⊞ Yellow/Green
- ▨ Green
- ⊟ Blue/Green
- ▥ Blue
- ▨ Blue/Violet
- ▦ Violet
- ◩ Red/Violet

Color Schemes Create Harmony

Looking at all the colors on the wheel can be confusing when you are choosing the colors with which you would like to work. Yet knowing and using the following color schemes, you will be able to choose the perfect ones. Keep in mind that the color shown represents that color in its pure form, as well as tints, shades, and tones of that color. For example, in a situation where red is suggested, pink (a tint of red) or burgundy (a shade of red) could be used.

If a tint or shade of a color is used for one flower choice, it should be used for all flowers chosen, with the exception of the monochromatic color scheme (Monochromatic color schemes will be described in more detail later in the chapter.) For example, if you have chosen a triadic color scheme of yellow, blue, and red, that same color scheme is depicted with tints of pale yellow, pale blue, and pink (this is great for spring or baby designs), as well as gold, navy blue, and burgundy (this suggests a very formal feeling).

Complementary Colors.

Colors that are located opposite each other on the color wheel are called *complementary colors*. This represents the brightest color scheme as the colors are opposing. Certainly you have used some of these schemes over and over: red and green at Christmas, yellow and violet at Easter. The complementary colors that can be used together are:

- ○ red and green
- ○ yellow and violet
- ○ orange and blue
- ○ yellow-green and red-violet
- ○ blue-green and red-orange
- ○ blue-violet and yellow-orange

Triadic Colors.

Three colors that are equally spaced on the color wheel are considered *triadic colors*. Triadic colors that can be used together are:

- ○ yellow, blue, and red
- ○ green, orange, violet
- ○ yellow-green, blue-violet, and red-orange
- ○ blue-green, red-violet, and yellow-orange

Analogous Colors.

An *analogous color scheme* consists of one primary or secondary color and the colors that are near it. This color scheme is flexible and may include colors a step or two away from the original color.

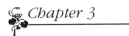

Monochromatic Colors.

Using a hue and tints and shades of that hue will produce a *monochromatic color scheme*. This is considered to be the most subtle and pleasing of all color combinations. Begin with any color, such as red, and combine it with a tint (pink) and a shade (deep red to burgundy).

Cool or receding colors are blues, greens, blue-violet, and violet. Warm or advancing colors are reds, red-violet, oranges, yellows, and yellow-green. Warm colors tend to excite and cheer people up. Cool colors are used for more formal settings and will soothe and calm people.

When deciding on which color combinations to use, begin with the existing colors in the room you wish to accent with a floral design. Start with a main color depicted in the room furnishings. Decide which other colors in the listed schemes would best bring out the nature of the room and feeling you wish to express in the room. In planning your designs, keep these basic rules and concepts in mind and color will be an extremely valuable tool for you.

CHAPTER 4

Round Designs

Since a circle is one of the first shapes we learn to draw as children, it is very memorable and pleasing to adult eyes. We like round wreaths on our walls and round flower arrangements on our tables. The look can encompass anything from a casual basket to a formal floral design.

MOUND DESIGNS

Mound arrangements are extremely versatile designs. They can be constructed in any-size round container from a very small bowl to the largest basket. The mound design is perfect when used in the center of the table as its beauty can be enjoyed from all sides.

Balance is of vital importance in creating a mound design. The arrangement must appear uniform in shape. The key is to keep materials equally spaced, with all extending an equal distance from the foam and container.

The height of the arrangement should be approximately $1^1/2$ to 2 times the *height* of the container. In cases where the container is wider than it is tall, or when you are using a nearly flat mat as a container, the approximate measurement is $1^1/2$ to 2 times the *width* of the container.

Follow the instructions in chapter 2 to judge the length each stem should be cut. Most importantly, do not pack the flowers too tightly together. By leaving the stems a bit longer, you will allow for additional space between and around the flowers. This will enable you to better appreciate each blossom.

Two methods can be used to create a mound table arrangement: the *counted flower method* and the *casual mass styling*. The counted flower method is used when the design consists mainly of flowers. The casual mass styling should be the choice if the finished design will consist of predominately light and airy dried materials.

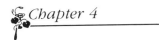
Counted Flower Method

The counted flower method is helpful in the purchase of materials because you can determine the exact number of flowers you will need to complete any given design. The flowers of this style should be equally spaced throughout to create a strong symmetrical appearance.

Always begin with the first row of flowers around the base of the arrangement. Since your design must be round in appearance, using the proper number of beginning flowers is important. Three flowers around the base is incorrect, since three flowers will create the look of a triangle, not a circle (FIG. 4-1). Four flowers give the appearance of a square or diamond instead of a circle, and therefore should be avoided (FIG. 4-2). The insertion of five flowers finally gives us the first circular appearance (FIG. 4-3). Six is the best number of flowers to use because it give the most circular appearance and is the easiest to equally space (FIG. 4-4).

The number of rows per arrangement will vary depending on the size of the flowers and the height of the desired design.

Fig. 4-1 (Top Left) Three flowers create the look of a triangle.

Fig. 4-2 (Top Right) Four flowers give a diamond- or square-shape appearance.

Fig. 4-3 (Bottom Left) The first circular appearance is achieved with five flowers.

Fig. 4-4 (Bottom Right) Six flowers surrounding the container is ideal.

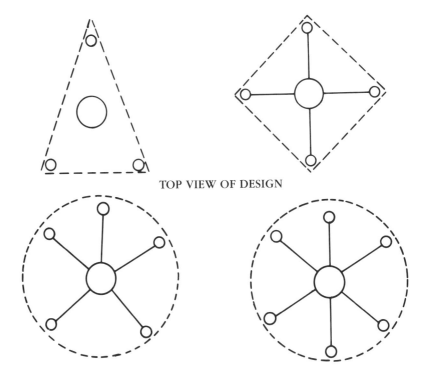

TOP VIEW OF DESIGN

Mound Design Using the Counted Flower Method

To construct the mound design with the counted flower method, you will need to use main flowers, which are the most prominent materials in the design and are inserted first; secondary flowers, which add color, texture, and depth to the design and are added after the main flowers; and one or more filler materials, which are designed to fill space and add additional color and texture.

You will need:

☐ One 4-inch-tall (10 cm) × 6-inch-wide (15 cm) wicker container

☐ 5-inch (12.5 cm) × 4-inch (10 cm) × 3-inch (7.5 cm) block Sahara foam

☐ Sphagnum moss to cover foam

☐ 16 red carnation stems—each stem contains one 3-inch (7.5 cm) flower head (main flowers)

☐ 5 stems yellow daisies—each stem contains three sections of two 2- inch (5 cm) daisies and a daisy bud (secondary flowers)

☐ 15 white 2-inch (5 cm) plastic eggs on picks

☐ 6 yards (5.5 cm) $^7/_8$-inch-wide (2 cm) blue gingham ribbon

☐ 2-oz. package preserved gypsophila

1. Prepare the container with foam and moss as described in chapter 1. Next, you will begin forming the basic arrangement with the main flowers.
2. Cut the stems of six carnations to 5 inches (12.5 cm). Insert two stems into the foam directly across from each other so they appear to cut the circle in half. All carnation heads should be approximately 2¹/₂ inches (6.5 cm) from the basket edge (FIG. 4-5).
3. Divide each side into three equal pieces by inserting two more flowers on either side, equally spaced between the first two flowers (FIG 4-6).

Fig. 4-5 (Below Left) Insert the first two flowers directly across from each other, parallel to the table edge.

Fig. 4-6 (Below Right) Equally space six flowers around the base.

The flowers in this row should be inserted parallel to the table so that the flower head overlaps the container edge when viewed from the side (FIG. 4-7). This treatment assures that the flowers and container appear as though they are one unit, rather than "floating above" the container. This is known as "softening" the container edge.

Fig. 4-7
Flowers should be parallel to the table edge.

Fig. 4-8 (Below Left)
Insert a single flower into the center of the design.

Fig. 4-9 (Below Right)
Three flowers are inserted at a 70-degree angle into the foam around the center flower.

4. Cut one stem 7 inches (17.5 cm) long and insert it straight up in the center of the design (FIG. 4-8).
5. You will use three flowers for the third row. Cut the stems of these flowers to 5 inches (12.5 cm) and insert at a 70-degree angle into the foam equally spaced around. (FIG. 4-9)
6. Cut six more carnation stems to 5 inches (12.5 cm). Insert equally spaced between the first row of six flowers and the row of three flowers. The stems should be inserted into the top of the foam and

angle approximately 30 degrees into the foam (FIG. 4-10). These flower heads should alternate above those in the first row and fall above the spaces between the first six flowers.

Fig. 4-10
Six flowers are inserted at a 30-degree angle into the foam.

This completes the insertion of your main flowers. Go through the following checklist before continuing with the secondary flowers.

Main flower checklist:

☐ Does the overall shape of your design appear round?

☐ Are all stems angled into the foam from the proper point of origin?

☐ Are the bottom row of flowers inserted parallel to the table and do they extend over the edge of the container?

☐ Is there ample room between and around the flowers for insertion of secondary and filler materials?

You are now ready to insert the daisies. These are considered the secondary flowers. The secondary flowers are important to:

○ add a different color or shade of the same color

○ form a contrast to the main flowers

○ add a variation of texture

○ help fill space

○ create a feeling of depth

Cut the stems of all the daisy sections so that their stem length is 6 inches (15 cm). Insert six in the first row, six in the second row, and three in the third row. No flower is inserted in the center, as there is already a flower in this location. You will be placing one daisy section in the space between each carnation in the first, second, and third rows. Each daisy section should be inserted at the same angle as the carnation in that row.

All daisies should be inserted 1 inch (2.5 cm) to 1½ inches (4 cm) deeper into the design than the carnations. This creates depth in the arrangement and helps each flower to be viewed and appreciated (FIG. 4-11). If any leaves remain on the daisy stem, cut them apart and insert deep in the center of the arrangement.

Fig. 4-11
The daisies are added for contrast, color, and texture change.

For different looks to the design, you can vary materials and flowers used. You can custom-create a design to fit any room styling with different choices of main and secondary flowers.

Follow this checklist before continuing with the filler materials.

Secondary Flower Checklist:

☐ Are the secondary flowers of a different color and texture than the main flowers?

☐ Are the secondary flowers inserted deeper into the arrangement than the main flowers?

☐ Is one secondary flower inserted between each main flower?

☐ Do the secondary flowers follow the same stem angle as the main flowers in that row?

When figuring the total numbers of flowers you will need to purchase consider this:

First row of main flowers	6
Second row of main flowers	6
Third row of main flowers	3
Fourth row of main flowers	1
Flower total	16 main
First row of secondary flowers	6
Second row of secondary flowers	6
Third row of secondary flowers	3
Fourth row of secondary flowers	0
Flower total	15 secondary

The filler materials are added last and achieve yet another change in color and texture designed to create a wonderful, interesting design to look at. Follow steps in chapter 2 to form 12 ribbon loop picks, each using 1/2-yard (45.5 cm) ribbon per pick and holding two loops. Insert these loops into the center of the design. Place them randomly throughout the spaces between the carnations and daisies.

Break the gypsophila into pieces 5 inches (12.5 cm) to 7 inches (17.5 cm) long, and insert evenly spaced throughout the design to fill any remaining bare spots. Be sure some of the shorter pieces are inserted deeper into the design.

Lastly add the eggs, placing one egg between each grouping of flowers in the bottom three rows (FIG. 4-12).

Fig. 4-12
Adding eggs into the design make it a perfect accent for the kitchen.

Mound Design Using the Casual Mass Styling

A container with or without a handle can be used to construct a mound in the casual mass styling.

You will need:

☐ One 9-inch-wide (22.5 cm) × 5-inch-high (12.5 cm) basket with a 10-inch-high (25.5 cm) handle

☐ 4-inch (10 cm) × 3-inch (7.5 cm) block of Sahara foam

☐ Spanish moss to cover foam

☐ Four stems of blue satin daisies—each stem contains three sections with two 2-inch (5 cm) flowers and a bud

☐ Two stems peach double blossoms—each stem contains six sprigs of four flowers each

☐ 2 yards (1.5 cm) $^{7}/_{8}$-inch-wide (2 cm) peach floral ribbon

☐ Half of a white 12-inch (30.5 cm) chenille stem

1. First prepare the container with foam and moss as described in chapter 1. Next, establish the mound shape with only the preserved gypsophila. Cut sprigs of gypsophila 6 inches (15 cm) long and insert to fill basket (FIG. 4-13). Refer to the point of origin drawing in chapter 3 to insert gypsophila at proper angles.

Fig. 4-13
First fill the basket with gypsophila in a rounded fashion.

2. Cut daisy sections from main stem so you have a 6-inch (15 cm) stem length. Insert one into the center of the basket. Insert four more equally spaced at a 45-degree angle into the foam around the first daisy. Figure 4-14 shows the top view of this step and FIG. 4-15 shows the side view.

3. Cut 6 more daisy sections with 6-inch (15 cm) stem lengths; insert these equally spaced around the basket edge (FIG. 4-16). They should be inserted parallel to the table edge, extending over the edge of the basket (FIG. 4-17). Any remaining flowers and leaves should be cut away from the main stem having 1-inch (2.5 cm) to 2-inch (5 cm) stems and inserted deep into the design near the foam.

4. Cut the two double blossom stems into single pieces, each with stem remaining, and insert throughout the design to fill space between daisies and gypsophila. (FIG. 4-18)

5. Form a floral bow, following the instructions in chapter 2. The bow should have 5-inch (12.5 cm) streamers and ten 2¹/₂-inch (6.5 cm) loops. Secure with chenille stem and wrap stem ends around basket handle to secure the bow to the front of the basket handle (FIG. 4-19).

Fig. 4-14 (Above Left) Top view of insertion of center and first row of four flowers.

Fig. 4-15 (Above Right) Side view showing flowers angled into foam.

Fig. 4-16 (Bottom Left) Insert six flowers equally spaced around the basket.

Fig. 4-17 (Bottom Right) The bottom row of flowers should rest over the edge.

Fig. 4-18 (Above Left) Insert double blossom sprigs between daisies.

Fig. 4-19 (Above Right) Finish the design by adding a bow.

OVAL DESIGN

The oval design, also known as the *centerpiece*, is a lovely accent to the center of any table, since it is equally beautiful when viewed from any side. It is best created in a long, low container. This design should not exceed 15 inches (38 cm) in height to allow guests seated at a table to converse easily. For a more formal look, candles can easily be inserted into the center of the arrangement.

As with the mound design, the oval is best when constructed using main flowers for impact; secondary flowers to add support, color, and texture changes; and filler materials to accent.

Step-by-Step Oval Design

You will need:

☐ One 10¹/₂-inch-long (27 cm) × 6-inch-wide (15 cm) × 1¹/₂-inch-tall (4 cm) green oval plastic container

☐ 8-inch-long (20 cm) × 2-inch-tall (5 cm) × 3-inch-wide (7.5 cm) block Sahara foam

☐ Spanish moss to cover foam

☐ Five stems of cream-colored lilies—each stem containing three sections with one 3-inch (7.5 cm) open flower and one 2-inch (5 cm) flower (main flowers)

☐ 16 stems pink miniature carnations each stem contains one 2-inch (5 cm) flower (secondary flowers)

☐ One green leaf bush containing twenty 4-inch (10 cm) leaves and twenty 3-inch (7.5 cm) leaves

☐ Five stems silk gypsophila—each stem containing 10 sprigs of four flowers each

For candle centerpiece variation, change the materials listed above to include: 14 miniature carnations instead of the 16 listed above, two 1-inch (2.5 cm) Lomey candle stakes, and two 10-inch (25.5 cm) taper candles.

1. Following the instructions in chapter 1, secure the foam into the container and cover with moss. Cut two lily sections from main stem with a measurement of 9 inches (22.5 cm) from tip of bud to end of stem. Insert one on each 6-inch (15 cm) end of container and insert into foam 1¹/₂ inches (4 cm). See FIG. 4-20. Flowers should be parallel to the tabletop with heads extending over the container edge (FIG. 4-21).

Fig. 4-20
Insert one lily on each end of the container.

Fig. 4-21
Flowers should be parallel to the table edge.

2. Cut six more lily sections 7 inches long (17.5 cm). Insert three on each side of the design equally spaced. Their stems should be inserted 1-inch (2.5 cm) into the foam, parallel to the table with the flower heads extending over the container edge (FIGS. 4-22 and 4-23).

3. Insert one 7-inch (17.5 cm) lily section, 1 inch (2.5 cm) into the foam and straight up in the center of the design. Figure 4-24 shows the side view of this step and FIG. 4-25 shows the top view.

Fig. 4-22
First row of flowers should rest over container edge.

Fig. 4-23
Bird's-eye view after six
more flowers are placed.

Fig. 4-24
Side view of flower inserted
into the center.

Fig. 4-25
Top view of central flower.

4. Six more 7-inch (17.5 cm) lily sections will be needed to complete the design. These should be inserted at a 45-degree angle into the top of the foam (FIG. 4-26). One should be placed directly above the two longest lily sections in the bottom row. Two more should be inserted equally spaced on each side of the design (FIG. 4-27). These will fall in the spaces between the bottom row of lilies.

Fig. 4-26
Insert six more flowers equally spaced at a 45-degree angle.

Fig. 4-27
Notice the top view of the newly placed flowers. In this photo the flowers are dark so they will be noticeable.

    Go through the following checklist before continuing with the secondary flowers.

Main Flower Checklist:

☐ From the top view of the design does the design appear oval in shape?

☐ Are the bottom row of flowers inserted parallel to the table and do they extend over the edge of the container?

☐ Is the center flower straight up and the middle row of flowers inserted at a 45-degree angle?

☐ Does ample room exist around the flowers for insertion of secondary and filler materials?

Now you are ready to insert the secondary flowers. These are chosen as a contrast to the main flowers to add a different color, as a variation of texture, and to create depth in the design. Miniature carnations were chosen as a secondary flower since their round shape will accent and contrast the shape of the lilies.

Cut the stems of all carnations to a length of 5 inches (12.5 cm). Insert eight flowers in the bottom row and six flowers in the middle row. These should be inserted approximately 1 inch (2.5 cm) to 1¹/₂ inches (4 cm) deeper into the design at the same stem angle as the lilies in the row (FIG. 4-28).

Fig. 4-28
Secondary flowers are added at the same stem angle as the main flowers.

Two carnations should be inserted into the top of the design. One should be placed on either side and approximately 1 inch (2.5 cm) lower than the central lily and each should be angled slightly into the arrangement. In FIG. 4-29 you will see the side view of this step and in FIG. 4-30 the top view is shown.

Fig. 4-29
Side view of the last two flowers inserted. They are darker in the photo so they will be noticeable.

Fig. 4-30
Top view including the last
two flowers; one located on
either side of central lily.

Different choices of main and secondary flowers will create many types of looks for the oval arrangement. Choose flowers that will accent the room or occasion for which the design is planned.

Follow this checklist before adding filler materials:

Secondary Flower Checklist:

☐ Are the secondary flowers of a different color and texture than the main flower?

☐ Are the secondary flowers inserted deeper into the arrangement than the main flowers?

☐ Is one secondary flower inserted between each main flower in the bottom and middle rows, with two flowers having been placed next to the top center flower?

☐ Do the secondary flowers follow the same stem angle as the main flowers in that row?

Fig. 4-31
Checklist design.

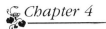
Filler Materials.

Green leaves are used as the first filler material in this design. They add a natural look to the arrangement, as well as help to fill space in the center of the design. Cut the leaves singly from the bush leaving 2-inch (5 cm) stems when possible. Insert all leaves deep into the design. The angle of the leaf stems should be the same as the flowers they are near. Be sure to bring some leaves down to the base of the container, placing them under the flowers in the first row (FIG. 4-32). If any leaf stem is too short for insertion, attach a wood pick to lengthen it.

Fig. 4-32
Insert leaves to fill space.

The silk gypsophila is added as a filler material to soften the look of the oval design. Cut the stems apart so that two sprigs remain on every stem. Insert these randomly throughout the design. The important aspect to remember is balance. The silk gypsophila should appear to be equally dispersed throughout the arrangement (FIG. 4-33).

To transform this oval into a candle centerpiece, remove the top two carnations and insert 1-inch (2.5 cm) Lomey candle stakes into the foam. Insert the candles into the cups (FIG. 4-34).

Fig. 4-33
Adding silk gypsophila gives the design a soft look.

Fig. 4-34
Used as a centerpiece, the oval design is very effective.

WREATHS

Wreathes can be created to fit any season or occasion. They can be designed to coordinate with any room in your home. Wreathes are extremely versatile and can be constructed utilizing a multitude of materials. In chapter 5 you will learn how to create wreaths with a crescent and a Hogarth accent. In chapters 7 and 10 special gift-giving wreaths will be explained. In this section we are dealing with wreaths designed to have decorations in an all-around fashion.

Review FIGS. 4-3 to 4-6 to see why it is important to design an all-around wreath with a minimum of five clusters around. This concept is even more important for a wall wreath, since you are viewing it straight on.

Round Wreath Step by Step

You will need:

☐ One 12-inch (30.5 cm) straw wreath

☐ A bundle of 15 straw flowers—each flower having a 2-inch to 2¹/₂-inch-wide (5 to 6.5 cm) head

☐ 5 yards (4.5 m) of ⁵/₈-inch-wide (1.5 cm) rust print ribbon

☐ 5 yards (4.5 cm) of ⁵/₈-inch-wide (1.5 cm) beige mini-dot ribbon with a lace edge

☐ 5 yards (4.5 m) of ⁵/₈-inch-wide (1.5 cm) yellow print ribbon

☐ 1-oz. package bleached preserved galaxy gypsophila

Fig. 4-35 (Top Left)
Begin the wreath design with five equally spaced clusters.

Fig. 4-36 (Top Right)
Secure the bow by placing a craft pin through the center portion.

Fig. 4-37 (Bottom Left)
Form a cluster of three bows between each cluster of straw flowers.

Fig. 4-38 (Bottom Right)
Fill the remaining portions of wreath with bows.

1. Begin by cutting the stems of all straw flowers to 1 inch (2.5 cm). Dip each in glue and insert into the straw wreath, forming five equally spaced clusters of three flowers each (FIG. 4-35).

2. Cut the 5-yard (4.5 m) pieces of three different ribbons into 1-yard (.9 m) pieces. Following instructions in chapter 2, form an eight-loop bow with one of the 1-yard (.9 m) lengths. The bow should have a 1½-inch-long (4 cm) loops and no streamers. Instead of securing the bow with a chenille stem or piece of cloth-covered wire, place a craft pin through the center of the bow, pulling it to the top of the pin (FIG. 4-36).

3. Insert the craft pin into the wreath snugly to attach the bow to the wreath. Form identical bows with each of the other two ribbons and cluster the three bows together between clusters of straw flowers (FIG. 4-37).

4. Continue forming bows and attach to the wreath until all five sections are filled (FIG. 4-38).

5. To soften the entire look of the wreath, break off 2 inch (5 cm) pieces of gypsophila and glue these pieces around the flowers and throughout the loops of the bows (FIG. 4-39). In FIG. 4-40, you will see the completed design.

Fig. 4-39 (Above Left) Glue small pieces of gypsophila throughout the bows and flowers.

Fig. 4-40 (Above Right) Completely fill wreath with gypsophila for a soft look.

MASS DESIGN

The mass designs of old were massive displays of multitudes of flowers designed to brighten areas in the homes of the wealthy. Generally speaking, they were one-sided arrangements designed to fit against a wall or in a corner. The ornate style of decorating is gone—so, too are the mass arrangements of old. Today's mass stylings depict a look of airy sophistication. More stylish than the mound arrangement, they add an upscaled look to our homes.

A mass arrangement is best used in the center of a table; however, it is also lovely when used on top of a china cabinet or the hearth of a fireplace. Its abundant use of various varieties of flowers makes it visually appealing.

For a contemporary look, choose a low bowl or basket-type container. An urn or other footed container will be perfect for a more old-fashioned feeling. As you create the mass design, remember that many different flowers can be substituted while still following the same basic steps to achieve spectacular effects.

Mass Design Step by Step

Several different types of flowers will be used to complete the mass design. You may substitute flowers and materials; however, keep in mind that this design looks best when many textures and shades of colors are used together. You will need:

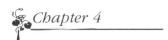

☐ One 11-inch (28 cm) deep green Lomey designer dish

☐ Half block Sahara foam

☐ Sphagnum moss to cover foam

☐ Three stems mauve azaleas—each stem containing two sections of three 2-inch (5 cm) flowers

☐ Two stems french blue lilies—each stem containing two sections of three 3-inch (7.5 cm) flowers

☐ Four stems eggshell carnations—each stem containing one 3-inch (7.5 cm) flower

☐ Two stems dark blue starburst flowers—each stem containing four sections of six 1-inch (2.5 cm) flowers

☐ Two stems eggshell starburst flowers—each stem containing four sections of six 1-inch (2.5 cm) flowers

☐ Two stems mauve zinnias—each stem containing three 2-inch (5 cm) open flowers and one bud

☐ 1/4 pound baby green eucalyptus

Fig. 4-41 (Below Left) The mass design begins with a single piece of eucalyptus in the center of the foam.

Fig. 4-42 (Below Right) Cut Each flower stem to the length indicated and insert as shown.

1. Prepare the container with foam and moss as described in chapter 1. Measure an 18-inch (45.5 cm) stem of eucalyptus and insert into the center of the foam block 2 inches (5 cm). See FIG. 4-41.

2. Three lines of flowers will form this mass design. All three of the lines pivot around the central eucalyptus piece. Each line will consist of a mixture of flower types at various stem lengths. Before inserting each flower stem into the foam, curve it slightly.

3. Follow the diagram in FIG. 4-42, cutting the indicated flower stems to

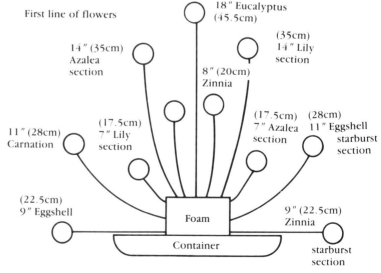

the designated length and inserting into the foam as shown in FIG. 4-43. All flowers should be inserted next to each other in a line. Figure 4-44 shows the side view, which emphasizes the side-by-side placement of the flowers. The next two lines when added to the design will form an ''X'' through the first line. Figure 4-45 shows the top view of the three lines as they will appear when the design is complete.

Fig. 4-43 (Above Right) Flowers inserted into the first row.

Fig. 4-44 (Above Left) The first row of flowers are inserted in a direct line.

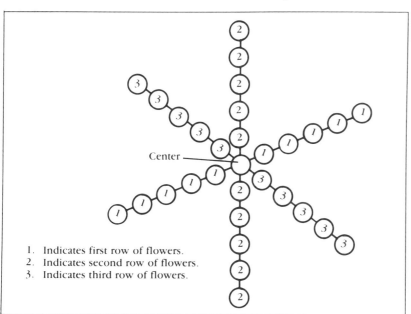

Center

1. Indicates first row of flowers.
2. Indicates second row of flowers.
3. Indicates third row of flowers.

Fig. 4-45 Top view of the position of the three lines.

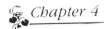

4. Follow the diagram in FIG. 4-46, cutting the indicated flower stems to the designated length and inserting into the foam. Figure 4-47 shows the top view of the second line when inserted. Figure 4-48 indicates the completed line from the top view. Figure 4-49 shows the stem length each remaining flower should be cut and its location in the design.

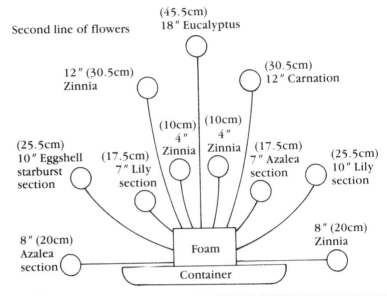

Second line of flowers

(45.5cm)
18″ Eucalyptus

12″ (30.5cm)
Zinnia

(30.5cm)
12″ Carnation

(10cm)
4″
Zinnia

(10cm)
4″
Zinnia

(25.5cm)
10″ Eggshell
starburst
section

(17.5cm)
7″ Lily
section

(17.5cm)
7″ Azalea
section

(25.5cm)
10″ Lily
section

Foam

8″ (20cm)
Azalea
section

8″ (20cm)
Zinnia

Container

Fig. 4-46
Cut the second row to the stem lengths indicated and place as shown.

Fig. 4-47 (Below Left)
Top view of insertion of the second row of flowers.

Fig. 4-48 (Below Right)
Top view of three rows of flowers.

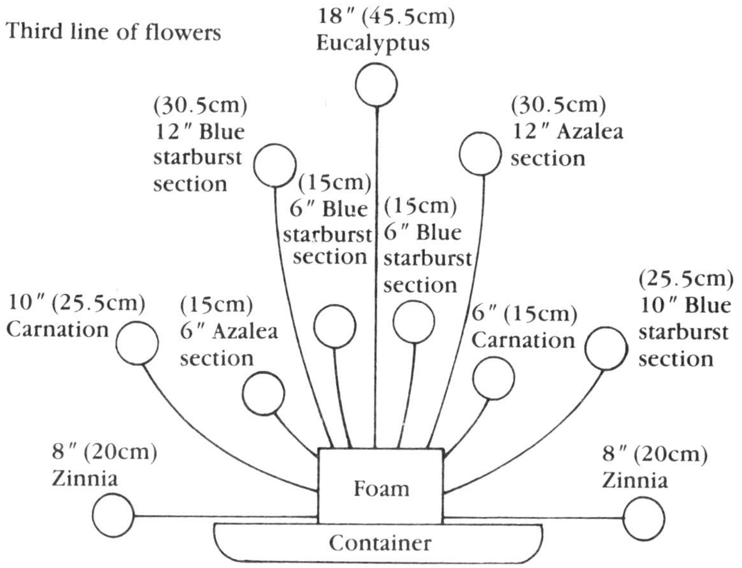

Third line of flowers

18" (45.5cm)
Eucalyptus

(30.5cm)
12" Blue
starburst
section

(30.5cm)
12" Azalea
section

(15cm)
6" Blue
starburst
section

(15cm)
6" Blue
starburst
section

10" (25.5cm)
Carnation

(15cm)
6" Azalea
section

6" (15cm)
Carnation

(25.5cm)
10" Blue
starburst
section

8" (20cm)
Zinnia

Foam

8" (20cm)
Zinnia

Container

Fig. 4-49 (Left)
Stem length cutting chart of
third row of flowers.

5. After the addition of all three lines, the design will look like that shown in FIG. 4-50. To fill any empty spots in the design, use the remaining eucalyptus. Break pieces away from the bundle. Remove the bottom leaves so that 2 inches (5 cm) of the end of the stem is clean.

Fig. 4-50 (Left)
The mass design after three
rows of flowers have been
inserted.

Cut the eucalyptus stem end at an angle and insert into the foam (FIG. 4-51). Use 6-inch (15 cm) to 8-inch (20 cm) pieces throughout the inside center and 10-inch (25.5 cm) to 12-inch (30.5 cm) pieces around the outside.

6. Cut the remaining two stems of starburst flowers apart into sections and insert in remaining bare spots throughout the design. Use shorter stems in the center and longer ones to the outside edges. Notice that the completed design in FIG. 4-52 has a feeling of openness, yet looks full and abundant.

Fig. 4-51 (Above Left) Insert stems of eucalyptus to fill space.

Fig. 4-52 (Above Right) Complete the airy feeling of the design with the addition of starburst flowers.

Curved Designs

*T*he crescent and Hogarth (or S-curve) are the arrangement styles that fall into the category of curved designs. All flowers that are inserted should appear to be part of curved lines rather than straight lines to achieve the proper overall look for the design. The eye of the viewer should be led along a line that prints a letter—a C for a crescent design and an S for the Hogarth or S-curve. Either of these designs can be formed as a table arrangement or a wall piece. They look especially nice when a table and wall design are combined together.

CRESCENT DESIGNS

There are many lovely uses for a crescent design. It works well on a table or mantle when its outline repeats the outline of an oval mirror or picture that has been placed behind it. A more open version accents a figurine or candle placed within or behind the design.

Low containers that are round, square, or rectangular are good choices for creating the crescent. The foam placed in the container should be approximately four fingers high, instead of two, to allow for the angle of the stems needed. The foam should be placed near the right side of the container if the tallest part of the crescent design is on the right-hand side, and near the left side if the tallest portion is on the left side. Creating a wall crescent is easy, since you will be following the natural curved shaped of the wreath.

Your flower choices should include a main flower, a secondary flower to add color and texture change, and a filler flower or material. Always begin with the main flowers in the design.

Crescent Table Design

You will need:

☐ One 11-inch (28 cm) Lomey designer dish
☐ One 6-inch (15 cm) × 3-inch (7.5 cm) × 2-inch (5 cm) Sahara II foam

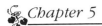

☐ 1-ounce package Spanish moss

☐ 10 carnations with 3-inch (7.5 cm) heads

☐ Eight roses with 2-inch (5 cm) heads

☐ Two stems of double blossom flowers with six sprigs of four flowers per stem

☐ U-shaped craft pins

☐ A hot-glue gun and sticks

1. Begin by glueing the foam to the back left side of the container. Cover it with moss and secure the moss with craft pins. Next, we will begin to form the letter C with the main flowers of the design—the carnations. In a crescent design the flowers represent the spokes of a wheel or the numbers on a clock, with all stems radiating into the foam (FIG. 5-1).

2. Cut the stem of the first carnation to a 12-inch (30.5 cm) length and gently curve the flower, inserting it into the back left corner on the side of the foam. Cut the second flower stem to a 6-inch (15 cm) length, curve gently, and insert into the right side of the foam (FIG. 5-2).

Fig. 5-1 (Left)
In a crescent design, flowers represent the spokes of a wheel or the numbers on a clock.

Fig. 5-2 (Right)
The first two flowers placed establish the crescent shape.

3. Cut the third carnation to a stem length of 8 inches (20 cm), curve gently, and insert into the left side of the design at the right front corner of the foam. Cut the fourth flower stem 5 inches (12.5 cm) and insert into the right side of the design at the front corner of the foam (FIG. 5-3).

4. Two more main flowers are added to complete the C from the front view. Insert a 6-inch (15 cm) flower left of center and a 5-inch (12.5 cm) flower right of center so that they fall in line with the other carnations (FIG. 5-4).

5. The next step is to reinforce the C shape with additional main flowers. Notice the flowers in FIG. 5-5 used for this purpose. For the design in the photograph, darker-colored flowers were used so that they would be more noticeable to you. The first flower stem is cut to 7 inches (17.5 cm) and inserted just to the right of the tallest carnation in the design. The second flower is cut to a length of 5 inches (12.5 cm) and inserted lower and to the left of the tallest carnation. The last two are cut to stem lengths of 3 inches (7.5 cm) and inserted into the top of the foam spaced between the flowers already in the design.

This completes the insertion of your main flowers. Go through the following checklist before continuing with the secondary flowers (FIG. 5-6).

Fig. 5-3 (Top Left) Add two flowers to continue the main line.

Fig. 5-4 (Top Right) A "C" forms the main line.

Fig. 5-5 (Bottom Left) Add flowers on either side to reinforce the main line.

Fig. 5-6 (Bottom Right) Follow the checklist before adding secondary flowers.

Main Flower Checklist:

☐ Have you formed the letter C with the main flowers?

☐ Are all the stems angled into the foam at the proper angles?

☐ Have you made certain that the tallest flower is *not* past the 12 o'clock mark and the opposite side of the crescent is *not* past the 4 o'clock mark?

☐ Is there ample room around the main flowers for insertion of secondary and filler materials?

Now you will be adding the secondary flowers for color and texture variation in the design. Your secondary flowers, the rosebuds, are inserted deeper into the design to create depth. The stem lengths of the roses, in order from the tallest flower around the curve to the opposite side are: 9 inches (22.5 cm), 7 inches (17.5 cm), 5 inches (12.5 cm), 5 inches (12.5 cm), and 4 inches (10 cm). These flowers should be inserted between the carnations in the original line of the C (FIG. 5-7).

Three more secondary flowers are inserted in order to reinforce the C shape. Two are placed further back in the design between the reinforcement carnations in that area. The longer stem is cut to 5 inches (12.5 cm) and placed near the taller side of the design. The shorter stem is cut to 3 inches (7.5 cm) and placed near the shorter side of the arrangement. The last secondary flower is cut to a 3-inch (7.5 cm) length and inserted on the outside of the tall curve of the design near the container edge (FIG. 5-8).

Follow the checklist before continuing with the filler materials.

Fig. 5-7 (Below Left) Place secondary flowers between the main flowers in the main line.

Fig. 5-8 (Below Right) Reinforce by adding more secondary flowers on either side of the main line.

Secondary Flower Checklist:

☐ Are the secondary flowers of a different color and texture than the main flowers?

☐ Are the secondary flowers inserted deeper into the design?

☐ Do the secondary flowers reinforce and repeat the C shape of the design?

The filler materials are added last and add yet another color and texture change to the design. Use the remaining leaves on the rose stems and the double blossom stems to fill in the design. Cut the double blossom sprigs apart so that some placements have two to three sprigs and others have only one. Insert these throughout the design to fill space. Insert the leaves in locations that may still look slightly bare.

In our finished piece, a 3-inch (7.5 cm) × 6-inch (15 cm) candle was placed behind the design to spotlight the shape of the design (FIG. 5-9).

Remember that you quickly create any style of crescent design by merely changing the materials you are using, but following the same procedure.

Fig. 5-9
A candle and filler flowers complete the crescent design.

Crescent Wallpiece

The materials you will need to complete this design include a 12-inch (30.5 cm) potpourri wreath as a base. If a prepared potpourri wreath is unavailable in your area, simply purchase a straw wreath, a 6-ounce package of potpourri, and white craft glue. Spread the white craft glue on the wreath, roll it in potpourri, and let dry. Fill in any bare spots when the wreath is dry.

Other materials needed include:

- ☐ 2 yards (1.8 m) of 1¹/₂-inch (4 cm) lace ribbon
- ☐ Five stems of roses—each stem containing one 2-inch (5 cm) open rose and one 1-inch (2.5 cm) bud
- ☐ Two stems of satin lily of the valley—each stem containing five sprigs and three leaves
- ☐ One chenille stem
- ☐ U-shaped craft pins and white craft glue
- ☐ 20-gauge stem wire
- ☐ Green floral tape

1. First form a bow with the ribbon having four 3-inch (7.5 cm) loops and two 12-inch (30.5 cm) streamers. Secure with the chenille stem and wrap the chenille stem ends around the center of the right side of the wreath, twisting behind to attach the bow to the wreath. Use craft pins to secure the streamers following a crescent pattern along the wreath side (FIG. 5-10).

2. Cut two rose stems to stem lengths of 8 inches (20 cm). Insert one into the wreath above the bow and the other into the wreath below the bow. These two should follow the curve of the wreath (FIG. 5-11).

3. Cut the other three stems so that the full rose has a 5-inch (12.5 cm) stem length. Reserve the rosebuds. Insert the three full rose stems in a

Fig. 5-10 (Below Left)
Establish the crescent shape with the bow and streamers.

Fig. 5-11 (Below Right)
Begin the form of the floral crescent with the longest two flowers.

Fig. 5-12 (Above Left)
Continue adding the main flowers to form the main line of the crescent.

Fig. 5-13 (Above Right)
Additional flowers are added on either side of the main line.

Fig. 5-14 (Left)
Lily of the valley sprigs and leaves add the finishing touches.

row equally spaced between the first two roses to form a continuous line (FIG. 5-12).

4. Cut the stems of the remaining buds to 3 inches (7.5 cm) and insert on either side of this central line to fill space (FIG. 5-13).

5. Wire each of the lily of the valley sprigs to a 3-inch (7.5 cm) length wire and insert randomly through the design to accent the roses. Glue the remaining leaves throughout to fill space (FIG. 5-14).

HOGARTH OR S-CURVE

William Hogarth was an eighteenth-century painter. He brought the S-curve or "Line of Beauty," as it was also known, to the attention of floral, arrangers of the period. This design style is still referred to as the Hogarth curve in many instances. It is a very upright and elegant design and therefore should be used in a place where the design is to be the focal point. Placing this design on a table in a corner or used next to a wallpiece will allow it to be featured and showcased.

A tall cylinder container is the best to use for the S-curve design. The S can be angled in the left or right direction. Neither the upper portion nor the lower sweep should extend past the central halfway point or you risk a loss of balance. Most commonly, the design looks best in its long, elegant state, instead of a short or very rounded styling. Wreaths are also useful containers when creating a wallpiece design.

Hogarth Table Arrangement

You will need:

☐ One 7-inch-tall (17.5 cm) × 3-inch-wide (7.5 cm) cylinder container

☐ 2-inch (5 cm) × 2-inch (5 cm) × 9-inch (22.5 cm) block Sahara II foam

☐ 1-ounce package moss

☐ Four stems eucalyptus with 12-inch (30.5 cm) leaf portion

☐ Two stems deep beige lilies—each stem containing two sections of three 2½-inch (6.5 cm) open flowers and one 1½-inch (4 cm) bud

☐ Three pencil cattails

☐ One stem rust double blossoms—each stem containing six sprigs

☐ U-shaped craft pins

☐ Hot-glue gun and sticks

☐ White craft glue

The foam should extend above the container approximately four fingers to allow the materials to be angled up into the design from the bottom (FIG. 5-15). The height of the flowers in this design are approximately 1½ to 2 times the height of the container.

Fig. 5-15 (Left)
The foam for the S-curve should be taller than for other designs.

Fig. 5-16 (Right)
Begin the line of the S with two pieces of eucalyptus.

Fig. 5-17 (Left)
The floral materials should be placed in front of the eucalyptus, but following the same line.

Fig. 5-18 (Right)
Continue adding additional lilies along the main line.

1. First you will establish the line of the design with two of the eucalyptus stems. Cut two stems to 12-inch (30.5 cm) lengths and curve gently. Insert one into the back left corner of the design curved upward and one into the front right side of the foam curved downward (FIG. 5-16).

2. The next step is to bridge this line by adding lilies. Cut one lily stem grouping to a 10-inch (25.5 cm) length and the other to an 8-inch (20 cm) length. Insert these so that they gently curve and follow the shape of the eucalyptus. The longer flower should extend upward, the shorter should extend downward (FIG. 5-17).

Fig. 5-19 (Left)
Side view shows the angle of the stems into the foam.

Fig. 5-20 (Right)
Pencil cattails are inserted between the flowers in the center of the design.

3. Two more lily sections should be used to completely bridge the line. Cut the upper stem to an 8-inch (20 cm) length and the lower stem to a 6-inch (15 cm) length and insert at an angle into the foam to visually connect the line. Figure 5-18 shows the front view of this completed step and FIG. 5-19 shows the side view, highlighting the angle of the inserted stems.

4. Next cut the cattail stems to 8 inches (20 cm) and insert them at an angle into the foam between the central lilies. Figure 5-20 shows the side view of this step.

5. Finish by adding the remaining filler materials. Cut the sections of double blossoms so that some stems have two sections and others have only one. Insert these throughout the design to fill space around the present flowers. Cut the last two eucalyptus stems to 4-inch (10 cm) and 5-inch (12.5 cm) lengths and insert into the center portion of the design. Figure 5-21 shows the front view of the finished design and FIG. 5-22 shows the side view of the same design.

Fig. 5-21 (Left) Silk double blossoms and smaller eucalyptus leaf stems fill the design.

Fig. 5-22 (Right) This side view shows the completed design.

Hogarth Wallpiece

You will need:

☐ One 11-inch (28 cm) pine needle wreath

☐ Two 12-inch (30.5 cm) eucalyptus stems

☐ Two stems beige lilies—each stem containing six 2-inch (5 cm) flowers and two 1½-inch (4 cm) buds

☐ One stem brown double blossoms with six sprigs per stem

☐ Six 1-inch (2.5 cm) to 2-inch (5 cm) pods on stems

1. Cut the stems of the eucalyptus to 2 inches (5 cm). Gently curve and insert one angled upward and the other angled downward into the wreath (FIG. 5-23).
2. Cut two lily sections to 9-inch (22.5 cm) stem length and insert one following the curve of the upper eucalyptus and one following the curve of the lower piece of eucalyptus (FIG. 5-24).

Fig. 5-23 (Left)
In forming an S-curve on a wreath, insert the first two stems into the wreath to begin to form the shape of the design.

Fig. 5-24 (Right)
Lilies are placed in front of the eucalyptus, along the same line.

3. Cut the remaining two lily groups to have 6-inch (15 cm) stems and insert into the wreath at a 45-degree angle to connect the S line of the design. Figure 5-25 shows the front view of this step and FIG. 5-26 shows the angle of the stems from the side.
4. Cut the double blossom sprigs apart singly and insert them throughout the design to fill space (FIG. 5-27).
5. The pods are used to add interest to the finished piece (FIG. 5-28). Cut the stems to 3-inch (7.5 cm) lengths and insert down the line of the S.

ADDITIONAL USES FOR CURVED DESIGNS

The following designs loosely follow the basics established above. Follow these steps to create additional arrangements or use your imagination and the basics taught above.

Fig. 5-25 (Left)
Continue to add lilies to establish the main line.

Fig. 5-26 (Right)
This photo shows the side view and the angle of the stems in the main line.

Fig. 5-27 (Left)
Silk double blossoms add a change of color as well as interest to the design.

Fig. 5-28 (Right)
The bulky look of the pods add a wonderful texture change.

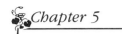

Feather Crescent Wreath

This wonderful, masculine design is subtle enough for a study, den, or recreation room, yet it has a spark of color and contrast to make it eye-catching (FIG. 5-29).

You will need:

☐ One 12-inch (30.5 cm) straw wreath

☐ 3-ounce bag Spanish moss

☐ Twelve assorted feathers in 6-inch (15 cm) to 12-inch (30.5 cm) lengths

☐ One lotus pod with 3-inch-diameter (7.5 cm) head

☐ Ten assorted pods with 2-inch (5 cm) to 3-inch (7.5 cm) heads

☐ 2 yards (1.8 m) 3-inch-wide (7.5 cm) blue gauze-like ribbon

☐ 2 yards (1.8 m) 1-inch-wide (2.5 cm) natural gauze-like ribbon

☐ One chenille stem

☐ U-shaped craft pins

1. Secure the Spanish moss to the wreath by inserting craft pins through the moss and into the wreath. Completely cover wreath in this fashion.
2. Insert the feathers in a line to establish the crescent shape on the side of the wreath.

Fig. 5-29 (Below Left) The feathers in this crescent wreath add a masculine feel to the design.

Fig. 5-30 (Below Right) A romantic crescent cascades off a wicker heart design.

3. Cut the stem of the lotus pod to 2 inches (5 cm) and insert into the center of the design.

4. Form a bow with the 3-inch (7.5 cm) ribbon, having eight 3-inch (7.5 cm) loops. Also form a bow with the 1-inch (2.5 cm) ribbon having eight 2¹/₂-inch (7.5 cm) loops. Insert these into the center of the design to fill space.

5. Cut the stems of the pods 2 inches (5 cm) to 4 inches (10 cm) in length. Insert throughout the feathers, ribbon, and other pods, staying within the crescent shape.

Romantic S-Curve Wall Heart

This design is perfect as a wallpiece for any style of home decorating—simply change colors to match the decor. By using the colors of red and white, you can make this an ideal gift for Valentine's Day (FIG. 5-30).

You will need:

☐ One 11-inch-wide (28 cm) × 2¹/₂-inch-deep (6.5 cm) vine heart basket

☐ One 2-inch-square (5 cm) block of Sahara II foam

☐ Small amount of Spanish moss to cover foam

☐ Four stems of silk needlepoint ivy—each stem measuring 9 inches (22.5 cm) in length

☐ 17 white satin carnations with 2-inch-wide (5 cm) heads

☐ 10 peach rosebuds with 1-inch (2.5 cm) heads

☐ 10 blue rosebuds with 1-inch (2.5 cm) heads

☐ Hot-glue gun and sticks

☐ U-shaped craft pins

1. Glue the foam at the bottom point of the heart resting on the left side of the basket. Cover with moss and secure with craft pins.

2. Glue one 9-inch (22.5 cm) length of ivy along the basket edge above the foam and a second one along the basket edge below the foam. The second one will cascade over the edge of the basket.

3. Remove the stems from 10 carnations and glue the heads along the ivy and the edge of the basket to establish the main line. Cut the remaining stems to 2-inch (5 cm) lengths and insert into the foam to reinforce the shape of the design.

4. Accent with the rosebuds. Remove the stems of some of the flowers and glue between the carnations on the ivy. Use 2-inch (5 cm) stem lengths for the remaining flowers and insert throughout the carnations in the center of the design. Alternate the colors as you go.

5. Cut the remaining ivy stems apart into 3-inch (7.5 cm) to 5-inch (12.5 cm) lengths and insert throughout the carnations in the center of the design.

Crescent Christmas Horn Design

Musical notes bring fond holiday memories. The pine in this design accents and reinforces the shape of the large musical instrument in the center (FIG. 5-31).

You will need:

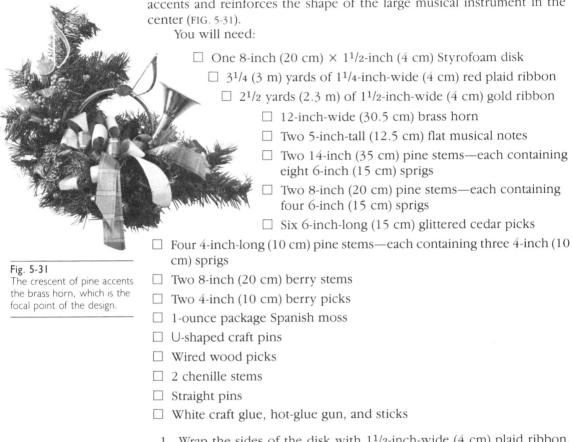

- ☐ One 8-inch (20 cm) × 1¹/₂-inch (4 cm) Styrofoam disk
- ☐ 3¹/₄ (3 m) yards of 1¹/₄-inch-wide (4 cm) red plaid ribbon
- ☐ 2¹/₂ yards (2.3 m) of 1¹/₂-inch-wide (4 cm) gold ribbon
- ☐ 12-inch-wide (30.5 cm) brass horn
- ☐ Two 5-inch-tall (12.5 cm) flat musical notes
- ☐ Two 14-inch (35 cm) pine stems—each containing eight 6-inch (15 cm) sprigs
- ☐ Two 8-inch (20 cm) pine stems—each containing four 6-inch (15 cm) sprigs
- ☐ Six 6-inch-long (15 cm) glittered cedar picks
- ☐ Four 4-inch-long (10 cm) pine stems—each containing three 4-inch (10 cm) sprigs
- ☐ Two 8-inch (20 cm) berry stems
- ☐ Two 4-inch (10 cm) berry picks
- ☐ 1-ounce package Spanish moss
- ☐ U-shaped craft pins
- ☐ Wired wood picks
- ☐ 2 chenille stems
- ☐ Straight pins
- ☐ White craft glue, hot-glue gun, and sticks

Fig. 5-31
The crescent of pine accents the brass horn, which is the focal point of the design.

1. Wrap the sides of the disk with 1¹/₂-inch-wide (4 cm) plaid ribbon, pinning ends to secure.
2. Attach horn to center of disk by cutting 4-inch (10 cm) lengths of chenille stem, forming into a U shape and placing over horn and into foam. For extra security, place craft pins in same manner over horn, but dip pin ends in white craft glue first.
3. Cover foam with moss around horn and secure moss to foam with craft pins.
4. Cut stem of 14-inch (35 cm) pine stems to 2 inches (5 cm), dip in glue, and insert one behind horn mouthpiece on left side of design curved upward. Insert second one in front of horn on right side of design parallel to table.
5. Cut stems of 8-inch (20 cm) pine to 2-inch (5 cm) lengths and insert one in front of pine on left side of design. Insert second one at base

of pine on right side in front of center of horn. These two pine pieces should be nearly touching and form outline of crescent shape.

6. Cut cedar pick stems to 2-inch (5 cm) length and insert three across front of design, filling space on foam base. Insert three behind horn, equally spaced, covering foam.

7. Cut stems of 4-inch (10 cm) pine to 1-inch (2.5 cm) length and insert two in front of design between glittered cedar and two behind horn between glittered cedar.

8. Cut stems of longer berries to 2 inches (5 cm). Curve one stem gently and insert in front of pine on left side following curve. Insert the other on right side, resting on top of pine.

9. Cut stems of smaller berries to 1 inch (2.5 cm) and insert one in front, centered between longer berry stems, and other centered behind horn.

10. Glue one musical note to curve of horn and the second above and to left, attaching it to the pine and berry spray.

11. Form a bow with the 1¹/₂-inch-wide (4 cm) plaid ribbon having two 10-inch (25.5 cm) streamers and eight 3-inch (7.5 cm) loops.

12. Using gold 1¹/₂-inch-wide (4 cm) ribbon, form two 10-inch (25.5 cm) single streamers on wood picks and insert into foam near plaid streamers. Form eight single loops on wood picks, each measuring 4 inches (10 cm), and insert randomly throughout plaid bow loops.

Inverted Basket Crescent

The crescent is used in a new way in this cute basket design. The basket lid acts as a filler for the back of the design (FIG. 5-32).

Fig. 5-32
An inverted crescent design is formed in a wicker basket.

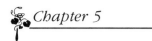

You will need:

☐ One 6-inch (15 cm) round willow basket with lid

☐ Four stems blue satin roses with a 3-inch (7.5 cm) open, 2-inch (5 cm) open, and 1-inch (2.5 cm) bud per stem

☐ Three stems ivory satin double blossoms with six sprigs per stem

☐ One stem of English Ivy containing three 12-inch (30.5 cm) ivy sections

☐ $1/2$ block Sahara II foam

☐ 1-ounce package Spanish moss

☐ U-shaped craft pins

☐ Hot-glue gun and sticks

1. Glue foam to inside of basket, cover with moss, and secure with pole pins.
2. Insert the lid slightly between the back of the foam and the back of the basket and glue in place.
3. Follow the directions for the crescent wreath above to complete the design. Begin by inserting two 9-inch (22.5 cm) rosebud stems, angling downward on either side of the wicker container. Continue inserting roses across the front to form the main line. Insert the final flowers above and below this main line to reinforce the line of the design.
4. Cut the double blossom stems into single sprigs and cut the ivy into smaller pieces. Insert both around the roses to fill space.

Candle Crescent

Easily constructed, this elegant crescent design is a perfect accent to the candle contained within (FIG. 5-33).

You will need:

☐ One 6-inch (15 cm) green Lomey designer dish

☐ $1/4$ block Sahara II foam

☐ Nine single stems of silk peach freesia

☐ Three stems white silk camellias with two 2-inch (5 cm) open flowers and one bud per stem

☐ Five stems silk ming fern with 12-inch (30.5 cm) ivy portions

☐ One 3-inch (7.5 cm) × 12-inch (30.5 cm) white candle

☐ One 3-inch (7.5 cm) Lomey candle stake

☐ 1-ounce package moss

☐ U-shaped craft pins

☐ Hot-glue gun and sticks

Fig. 5-33
Freesia and camellia are a lovely contrast to the large decorative candle.

1. Secure foam to container, cover with moss and insert craft pins to secure.
2. Insert Lomey candle stake into center of foam and place candle inside.
3. Floral design should be created around the candle, allowing for materials to accent candle. Follow basic crescent design above for outline of technique. Begin by inserting ming fern and freesia to form the C shape needed.
4. Fill in deeper in the design with the camellias for accent.
5. Cut remainder of ming fern into smaller pieces and insert around the flowers in the center of the design.

Crescent Fruit Basket

Gift baskets make wonderful gifts. The concept of the crescent is used in this design to accent the handle and front of the basket (FIG. 5-34).

You will need:

☐ One 12-inch (30.5 cm) wide whitewashed peach basket

☐ 4 yards (3.5 m) of 2-inch-wide (5 cm) natural gauze-like ribbon

☐ Seven peach rosebuds with 1-inch-wide (2.5 cm) heads

☐ Two 9-inch (22.5 cm) lengths ivy

☐ 1-ounce package iridescent shredded grass

☐ One eggshell chenille stem

☐ Assorted goodies to fill basket

☐ Hot-glue gun and sticks

Fig. 5-34
The crescent floral portion accents the handle of this gift basket.

1. Form a 10-loop bow with 2-inch (5 cm) to 3-inch (7.5 cm) loops and 12-inch (30.5 cm) streamers.
2. Secure the bow to the left side of the basket with the chenille stem. Curl the streamers around the handle and glue the end in place. Twirl the other streamer across the front of the basket and glue in place.
3. Glue one ivy stem upward through the bow and one across the front of the basket.
4. Remove the roses from their stems and glue in a crescent fashion through the bow loops and along the streamers.

Line Designs

*L*ine designs consist of any arrangement style that has strong straight lines either vertical, horizontal, or diagonal—unlike the curved lines we find in crescents and S-curves. We will be discussing two types of line designs: the vertical and the ⊤ design.

VERTICAL ARRANGEMENT

Vertical arrangement is a very dynamic arranging style since it emphasizes a strong upward thrust. These arrangements are usually designed in tall, narrow containers, which accent the height of the arrangement. Appropriate materials must be used to establish the vertical line. These line materials include any long, narrow materials, whether floral, dried, or other. Few main flowers are used and must be placed in a vertical line, with one flower slightly lower than each above it. More space should be used between the flowers at the tallest portion, with less space between those closer to the focal point of the design, which is located at the container edge.

A common mistake in a vertical arrangement is to overdevelop the focal area. The materials used should not extend very far past the confines of the sides of the container. The best thing to remember is: Keep it simple!

Vertical Arrangement Step by Step

Few materials are needed; however, the strength of the line achieved is noticeable. The height of the arrangement is $1^{1}/_{2}$ to 2 times the height of the container.

Remember as you make this design that you can change the materials you are using to create a whole new look and feel to the basic vertical technique.

You will need:

☐ One 7-inch-tall (17.5 cm) × 4-inch-wide (10 cm) eggshell ceramic container

☐ 3-inch (7.5 cm) × 3-inch (7.5 cm) × 3-inch (7.5 cm) block Sahara II foam

☐ 1-ounce package Spanish moss

☐ Three stems silk heather, with heather portion measuring 8 inches (20 cm)

☐ One stem cream fuji mum containing three flower heads, measuring 1 inch (2.5 cm), 2^1/$_2$ inches (6.5 cm), and 4 inches (10 cm)

☐ Ten leaves 3 inches (7.5 cm) to 4 inches (10 cm) long

☐ Hot-glue gun and sticks

☐ U-shaped craft pins

☐ Wired wood picks

1. Glue the foam into the container, cover with moss, and secure the moss with craft pins. Cut the first heather stem to a 14-inch (35 cm)

Fig. 6-1 (Left)
The tallest flower in the vertical design should be 1^1/$_2$ to 2 times the height of the container.

Fig. 6-2 (Middle)
The placements in a vertical design should not extend over the sides.

Fig. 6-3 (Right)
Add the first main flower in front of the first line flower in the design.

length and insert it into the center back of the foam. This will be the tallest line flower and establishes the height of the design (FIG. 6-1). When measuring your own designs, this flower should be 1¹/₂ to 2 times the container height.

2. Cut the second heather stem to 11-inch (28 cm) lengths and insert into the back left corner of the foam, slightly in front of the first. Cut the third heather stem to a 9-inch (22.5 cm) length and insert into the right side of the design. Notice in FIG. 6-2 that all three flowers are at different heights and the stems are placed vertically in the design instead of at an angle, as is appropriate in other design styles.

3. Cut the smallest fuji mum flower so it has an 8-inch (20 cm) stem length. Insert it into the center of the design just in front of the first heather stem (FIG. 6-3).

4. Cut the medium-sized fuji mum stem to a length of 6 inches (15 cm) and place it slightly to the left of the first fuji stem. Instead of placing this flower straight up as the others in the design, angle it slightly into the design so that you see more of the front of the flower from the front of the arrangement (FIG. 6-4).

Fig. 6-4 (Left)
The second main flower should be located below and to one side of the first.

Fig. 6-5 (Middle)
The third main flower should be located below and to the opposite side of the first flower.

Fig. 6-6 (Right)
Fill the base of the design with leaves.

5. Cut the largest fuji mum so it has a 4-inch (10 cm) stem and then insert it slightly to the right of the central fuji. This flower should also be inserted at an angle so that it slightly rests on the container edge (FIG. 6-5).

6. Attach the leaves individually to wood picks or floral tape to lengths of stem wire. Then insert around the base of the design to fill space (FIG. 6-6).

T-Wreath Design

The T style can be created on a wreath, in which case you clearly see the letter "T" formed. It can also be created in a flat container. When in a container, the design is created upside down so that the flat top part of the letter is the longest portion of the design and is resting on the container edge. In this case, it is called an *inverted T design*.

You will need:

☐ One 12-inch (30.5 cm) excelsior wreath

☐ Six stems silk heather with 8-inch (20 cm) flower portions

☐ Two stems mauve fuji mums—each stem containing three flowers measuring 1 inch (2.5 cm), 2¹/₂ inches (6.5 cm), and 4 inches (10 cm) and having ten leaves

☐ Wired wood picks

☐ White craft glue

☐ U-shaped craft pins

1. Begin the design by establishing the outline or letter T. Cut two stems of heather to a stem length of 10 inches (25.5 cm) and insert them end-to-end at the top of the wreath with the stems 1 inch (2.5 cm) apart. Dip these stems into white craft glue before insertion. Insert a craft pin through the flower stem and into the wreath ¹/₂ way down the stem (FIG. 6-7).

2. Three heather stems are used to establish the lower portion of the T. Cut one heather stem to a length of 12 inches (30.5 cm), one to a length of 9 inches (22.5 cm), and one to a length of 8 inches (20 cm). You may need to trim away some of the bottom flowers from the shorter two stems so that you have at least 1 inch (2.5 cm) of clear stem to insert into the wreath. Insert these three flowers into the wreath as shown in FIG. 6-8.

3. Next, place three fuji mums into the wreath, one on each extension of the T. The top left flower is a medium-sized flower measuring 7 inches (17.5 cm). The top right flower is a small flower measuring 7 inches (17.5 cm). The lower flower is a small flower measuring 9 inches (22.5 cm). See FIG. 6-9 for proper placement.

4. Add three more mums in the focal area of the wreath in a triangular fashion. The upper left flower is a large flower stem measuring 4 inches (10 cm). The upper right flower is a medium flower stem measuring 4 inches (10 cm). The lower flower is a large flower stem measuring 6 inches (15 cm). Figure 6-10 will show you the proper placement of these three flowers.

5. Cut the remaining heather stem into thirds, each third having 1-inch of (2.5 cm) bare stem to insert into the wreath. One heather piece is inserted between the two flowers at the top of the wreath. Place one of each of the remaining two pieces on either side of the flower below the two top flowers. Attach all the leaves to wired wood picks and insert them throughout the design to fill space and reinforce the look of the T.

Fig. 6-7 (Top Left)
Insert first two stems of the T into the top of the wreath.

Fig. 6-8 (Top Right)
Form the lower portion of the T with three line flowers.

Fig. 6-9 (Bottom Left)
Begin at the outer points to add the main flowers.

Fig. 6-10 (Bottom Right)
Fill in the center with three main flowers in a triangle.

ADDITIONAL LINE DESIGNS

The following line design variations will make wonderful gifts or perfect accents for your home. Change the flowers, colors, or containers to create new exciting looks.

Candy Dish

The vertical look of the flowers in this design accents the dish of candy, which is the main gift in this arrangement (FIG. 6-11).

You will need:

- [ ] One 11-inch (28 cm) Lomey designer dish
- [ ] One Lomey small caged foam
- [ ] One stem mauve fuji mums with 10 leaves, and three flowers measuring 1 inch (2.5 cm), 2½ inches (6.5 cm), and 4 inches (10 cm)
  - [ ] One stem pink daisies containing eight 1-inch (2.5 cm) flowers
  - [ ] Two stems white silk baby's breath
  - [ ] 1-ounce package iridescent shredded grass
  - [ ] Hot-glue gun and sticks
    - [ ] U-shaped craft pins
      - [ ] Candy of your choice to fill dish

1. Glue the foam cage into the center of the designer dish, cover with the shredded grass, and secure with craft pins.
2. First insert the three fuji mums, with the tallest being 12 inches (30.5 cm), the second flower being 9 inches (22.5 cm), and the shortest being 6 inches (15 cm).
3. Cut the daisies and baby's breath to stems of varying lengths between 10 inches (25.5 cm) and 4 inches (10 cm), and insert around the fuji mums to fill space.

Fig. 6-11
A vertical design accents a gift of candy.

Potpourri Gift-Giving Basket

The wonderful aroma of the potpourri decoratively displayed in this basket adds a special touch to the design (FIG. 6-12).

You will need:

- [ ] Wicker basket with a 10-inch-wide (25.5 cm) × 4-inch-tall (10 cm) base and a 12-inch-tall (30.5 cm) handle

- ☐ 1-pound package peach-scented potpourri
- ☐ 3¹/₂ yards (3 m) of ¹/₂-inch-wide (1.2 cm) peach plaid ribbon
- ☐ 3¹/₂ yards (3 m) of ¹/₂-inch-wide (1.2 cm) blue calico ribbon
- ☐ 3¹/₂ yards (3 m) of ¹/₂-inch-wide (1.2 cm) natural calico ribbon
- ☐ Six pencil cattails
- ☐ One package natural ting ting (approx. 36 pieces)
- ☐ 1-ounce package natural gypsophila
- ☐ One floral bush containing four 4-inch (10 cm) rust zinnias, two 3-inch (7.5 cm) natural lilies, two azalea stems, two daisy stems, and two silk gyp stems
- ☐ One small Lomey caged foam
- ☐ Wood picks
- ☐ Cloth-covered wire
- ☐ Hot-glue gun and sticks

Fig. 6-12 (Below Left) This potpourri gift basket is a lovely accent for almost any room.

Fig. 6-13 (Below Right) Line diagram for stem lengths.

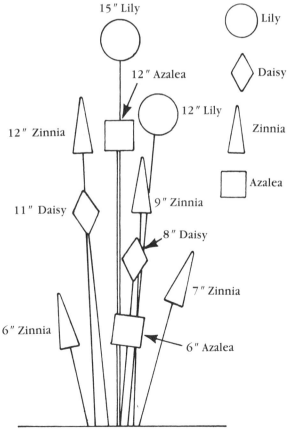

1. Glue the caged foam into the left side of the basket.
2. Cut 1¹/₂-yard (1.3 m) lengths of each of the ribbons. Staple or wire the ends of all three together and braid the entire length. Glue this braid around the top edge of the basket.
3. With the remaining ribbon, form a bow, with each ribbon having eight 3-inch (7.5 cm) loops. Wire all three together and wire to the right handle of the basket. Wrap the remaining ribbon streamers around the handle and glue at the opposite end.
4. Follow diagram in FIG. 6-13 on p. 77 to cut the flower stems the appropriate length and insert into the foam for the floral design. Cut the stems of the flowers to the following lengths and insert into the foam in a vertical fashion: *lily*—15 inch (38 cm), 12 inch (30.5 cm); *zinnia*—12 inch (30.5 cm), 9 inch (22.5 cm), 7 inch (17.5 cm), 6 inch (15 cm); *azalea*—12 inch (30.5 cm), 6 inch (15 cm); *daisy*—11 inch (28 cm), 8 inch (20 cm).
5. After completion, insert pieces of the gypsophila around and through to fill space.
6. Insert the cattails at various heights to create interest.
7. Form loops with the ting ting by bringing the ends together and wiring them to wood picks. Insert these loops around the base of the design. Insert individual pieces of ting ting vertically throughout the floral design.
8. Fill basket with the potpourri, covering the foam.

Vertical Easter Basket Design

The vertical design use here to accent the side of this Easter basket is a very effective way of highlighting the plush lamb contained within (FIG. 6-14).

You will need:

☐ One 11-inch (28 cm) lavender Lomey design dish

☐ 3 yards (2.7 m) untwisted mauve paper ribbon

☐ 1¹/₂ yards (1.3 m) mauve whitewashed untwisted paper ribbon

☐ One small Lomey caged foam

☐ 1-ounce package iridescent shredded grass

☐ One stem silk forsythia with a 12-inch (30.5 cm) stem

☐ Five stems purple silk rosebuds with 1¹/₂-inch (4 cm) heads

☐ Three stems pink daisies with six 1-inch (2.5 cm) flowers per stem

☐ Five silk pothos leaves, each measuring 3 inches (7.5 cm)

☐ 3 yards each pink and purple narrow curling ribbon

☐ Cloth-covered wire

☐ Hot-glue gun and sticks

☐ 12-inch (30.5 cm) length 18-gauge wire

☐ Small plush lamb or other toy

1. Cut six 18-inch (45.5 cm) lengths of mauve untwisted paper ribbon and three pieces the same length from the whitewashed paper ribbon. Each length of the braid will be formed from three pieces of paper ribbon held together.

2. Use a 6-inch (15 cm) length of cloth-covered wire to secure the nine ends of untwisted paper ribbon along with the length of 18-gauge wire and braid together. Follow FIG. 6-15 to see the braid forming. Use cloth-covered wire at the other end to secure the braid.

3. The ending braid should measure 12 inches (30.5 cm). Glue one end of the braid on either side of the designer dish, holding in place until dry.

4. Glue the foam cage to the back left side of the dish, cover with iridescent grass using craft pins to secure in place.

5. Form the vertical design in the foam following the basic instructions earlier in this chapter as a guideline. The tallest forsythia is 14 inches

Fig. 6-14 (Left)
The vertical arrangement in this design creates a perfect background for the plush animal.

Fig. 6-15 (Right)
Form the braided handle with nine lengths of paper ribbon and a piece of 18-gauge wire.

(45 cm), the tallest daisy is 12 inches (30.5 cm), and the tallest rose-buds is 10 inches (25.5 cm). The flowers become shorter as they reach the container, alternating as you go down.

6. The stems of the pothos leaves should measure approximately 1 inch (2.5 cm); these leaves should be placed around the bottom of the design to fill space and cover the foam base.

7. Form small bows with 18-inch (45.5 cm) streamers from the curling ribbons and attach at the location where the handle meets the dish to cover the join spot. Place the plush animal and perhaps some candy treats in the designer dish.

Double Vertical Spring Wreath

Follow the basic instructions for the vertical design earlier in this chapter and use the rules taught to assist you in the creation of this design. The design on the left side is fashioned to be slightly fuller (FIG. 6-16).

Fig. 6-16
A double vertical arrangement adorns a grapevine wreath.

You will need:

☐ One 12-inch (30.5 cm) grapevine wreath

☐ 1-ounce package Spanish moss

☐ Five ivy picks with six 3-inch leaves each

☐ Six purple irises

☐ Five stems apple blossoms with 14-inch (35 cm) floral portions

☐ Three stems pussy willows with 12-inch (30.5 cm) floral portions

☐ Six stems pink lilies with 2-inch (5 cm) open flowers

☐ One stem green onion grass

☐ White craft glue

1. Glue small amounts of Spanish moss on opposite sides of the grape-vine wreath. These will be the locations in which you insert the flowers. The flowers are inserted directly into the wreath with the vines providing support. Dip each flower stem into glue before insertion.

2. Cut the stems of the flowers for the design on the left side as follows and insert to form a vertical arrangement: *iris*—12 inch (30.5 cm), 10 inch (25.5 cm), 6 inch (15 cm), 4 inch (15 cm); *apple blossom*—14 inch (35 cm), 12 inch (30.5 cm), 10 inch (25.5 cm), 6 inch (15 cm); *pussy willow*—12 inch (30.5 cm), 10 inch (25.5 cm); *pink lilies*—14 inch (35 cm), 12 inch (30.5 cm), 10 inch (25.5 cm), 8 inch (20 cm), 6 inch (15 cm), 4 inch (10 cm). Place one onion grass and two ivy picks at the base of the design (FIG. 6-17).

3. Cut the stems of the flowers for the design on the right side as follows and insert to form a vertical arrangement: *iris*—8 inch (20 cm), 4 inch (10 cm); *apple blossom*—10 inch (25.5 cm), 7 inch (17.5 cm), 4 inch (10 cm); *pussy willow*—6 inch (15 cm), 3 inch (7.5 cm). Place one ivy pick at the base (FIG. 6-18).

4. Insert the remaining two ivy picks into the wreath halfway between the floral portions in the front and in the back of the design.

Fig. 6-17 (Left) Closeup of the left side of the spring wreath.

Fig. 6-18 (Right) Closeup of the right side of the spring wreath.

Fall T-Wreath

The T style of design is suggested in this abundant fall wreath (FIG. 6-19). You will need:

- [ ] One 14-inch (5 cm) grapevine wreath
- [ ] One 2-inch (5 cm) block Sahara II foam
- [ ] 1-ounce package Spanish moss
- [ ] 2 yards (1.8 m) 1½ inch (4 cm) wide fall-print ribbon
- [ ] Six stems fall leaves with 7-inch (17.5 cm) leaf portion
- [ ] Three stems berries with 8-inch (20 cm) berry portion
- [ ] 1-ounce package German statice
- [ ] One chenille stem
- [ ] U-shaped craft pins
- [ ] Hot-glue gun and sticks

Fig. 6-19
The deep, crisp colors of the Fall T-Wreath make it a beautiful accent for the season.

1. Glue the foam to the top center of the vine wreath. Cover it with moss and secure in place with craft pins.
2. First you must form the T with the fall leaves. Cut one leaf stem so it measures 10 inches (25.5 cm) and insert into the center of the wreath as the bottom portion of the T. Cut two more leaf portions so they measure 8 inches (20 cm) and insert one into the left side of the foam and one into the right side of the foam as either side and of the top of the T.
3. Cut the remaining leaf stems in half and insert four 4-inch (10 cm) pieces equally spaced across the top of the wreath connecting the two 8-inch (20 cm) stems. Insert the remaining pieces under the foam in the center of the wreath.
4. Cut one berry stem to 8 inches (20 cm) and insert on top of the leaf portion at the bottom of the wreath. Cut two more stems to 5 inches (12.5 cm) and insert one on either side of the foam to form the top portion of the T. Insert the remaining 3-inch (7.5 cm) berry pieces equally spaced around the top of the foam.
5. Form a bow with the ribbon having eight 3-inch (7.5 cm) loops and 8-inch (20 cm) streamers, secure with the chenille stem and insert into the center of the foam to fill space.
6. Break small pieces of statice and glue through the bow loops and among the leaves and berries.

Christmas Designs

*T*he Christmas holiday season is a perfect time for gift-giving florals. We also feel a need to decorate our own homes at this special time of the year. The following designs will get you started on your way.

CHRISTMAS TIN

This design (FIG. 7-1) is created in a diagonal fashion, but the construction techniques mirror those used in the basics of the oval design in chapter 4.

You will need:

☐ One 6-inch (15 cm) tall × 4¹/₂ inches (11.5 cm) wide holiday tin
☐ 8-inch-tall (20 cm) × 3-inch (7.5 cm) block Sahara II foam
☐ 1-ounce package Spanish moss
☐ Two stems holly with 7-inch (17.5 cm) portions of holly and berries
☐ Four stems holly with 3-inch (7.5 cm) portions of holly and berries
☐ Four 2-inch (5 cm) pinecones on stems
☐ Two frosted cedar stems with 10-inch (25.5 cm) sections
☐ Twelve frosted cedar stems with 4-inch (10 cm) sections
☐ Hot-glue gun and glue sticks, white craft glue
☐ U-shaped craft pins

1. Glue the foam into the tin and cover with moss, securing with craft pins.
2. Cut the ends of the 10-inch (25.5 cm) cedar stems to 2-inch (5 cm) lengths and insert one angled upward into the left side of the foam and one angled downward into the right side of the foam. If connected by an imaginary line, these two stems would resemble a diagonal line.
3. Cut the stems of the 4-inch (10 cm) cedar stems to 1 inch (2.5 cm) and insert six equally spaced in the front of the design and six in the back. These 12 stems should connect with the 10-inch (25.5 cm) stems and form a complete oval shape when viewed from the side.

Fig. 7-1 (Below Left)
This holiday tin design adds
a festive touch to the season.

Fig. 7-2 (Below Right)
The lid is glued in the center
of the foam surrounded by
pine.

4. Glue the lid of the can to the center of the foam in between the cedar stems (FIG. 7-2).

5. Cut the stems of the two 7-inch (17.5 cm) holly stems and insert them into the foam just above the two 10-inch (25.5 cm) cedar stems.

6. Cut the remaining four holly stems to 1-inch (2.5 cm) lengths; insert two in the front of the design below the tin lid and insert two into the back of the design at the same location.

7. Cut the stemmed cones to 2-inch (5 cm) lengths and place randomly throughout the design to fill any extra space.

TEDDY BEAR MOUND

This is a delightful design anyone would love. It is very simple and closely follows the instructions for the mound design in chapter 4 (FIG. 7-3).

You will need:

☐ One 4-inch-tall (10 cm) × 4-inch-wide (10 cm) ceramic teddy container

☐ 5-inch-tall (12.5 cm) × 3-inch-wide (7.5 cm) square block Sahara II foam

☐ 1-ounce package Spanish moss

- ☐ Sixteen 6-inch (15 cm) frosted glittered pine stems
- ☐ Nine 4-inch (10 cm) holly clusters containing packages, satin balls, and berries
- ☐ Twelve 5-inch (12.5 cm) candy canes on stems
- ☐ Six 2-inch (5 cm) flocked teddy bears on picks
- ☐ Hot-glue gun and sticks
- ☐ U-shaped craft pins

1. Glue the foam into the container and cover with moss, securing with craft pins.
2. Follow the basic instructions in chapter 4 for the mound design and insert the pine picks: six in the first row, six in the second row, three in the third row, and one in the center top.
3. Insert the package clusters: six in the first row and three in the second row.
4. The candy canes and teddy bears should be inserted randomly throughout the design in a pleasing fashion.

Fig. 7-3 (Above)
The teddy bears in the design reinforce the motif depicted on the container.

CHRISTMAS CANDLE CENTERPIECE

This lovely holiday centerpiece is a wonderful hostess gift. Create one to complement your own festive table. Refer to the instructions for a basic oval design in chapter 4 to assist you in constructing this piece (FIG. 7-4).

You will need:

- ☐ One 10-inch-long (25.5 cm) × 6-inch-wide (15 cm) × 2-inch-tall (5 cm) flat green container
- ☐ 8-inch-long (20 cm) × 2-inch-tall (5 cm) × 3-inch-wide (7.5 cm) block Sahara II foam
- ☐ 1-ounce package Spanish moss
- ☐ Three 1-inch (2.5 cm) Lomey candle stakes
- ☐ Two 10-inch (25.5 cm) red candles
- ☐ One 12-inch (30.5 cm) red candle
- ☐ Two 10-inch-long (25.5 cm) pine stems with seven 6-inch-long (15 cm) sprigs
- ☐ Ten 6-inch-long (15 cm) pine stems with six 3-inch-long (7.5 cm) sprigs
- ☐ Five cluster picks containing a package, pinecone, berries, and satin ball

☐ Five 6-inch-long (15 cm) holly berry picks

☐ Eight 3-inch-long (15 cm) holly berry picks

☐ Two 3-inch (7.5 cm) glittered cedar picks

☐ Two 3-inch (7.5 cm) gold fans on stems

☐ U-shaped craft pins

☐ Hot-glue gun and glue sticks

1. Glue the foam into the container, covering with moss and securing with craft pins.
2. Cut the stems of two 10-inch (25.5 cm) pine stems to 2 inches (5 cm) and insert one into each long end of the container.
3. Cut the stems of the ten 6-inch (15 cm) pine stems to 1 inch (2.5 cm) and insert five on either side of the container equally spaced. At this point an oval of pine should be formed around the container edge.
4. Insert the three candle cups equally spaced across the top of the foam.
5. In a second row above the pine, insert two cluster picks in one side of the arrangement placed under the two outside candles. Insert three on the other side of the design equally spaced across the arrangement. These stems should be cut to 2 inches (5 cm).
6. Cut the stems of the holly berries to 1 inch (2.5 cm) and insert one on each end of the arrangement and one between the clusters on the sides of the arrangement.
7. With the stems cut to 2 inches (5 cm), insert three glittered cedar picks around each of the outside candles to fill space and one below each holly berry pick on the ends of the design.
8. Insert two gold fans into the center front of the design as shown in FIG. 7-4.

Fig. 7-4
The candles in this design will add a warm feeling to the holiday season.

HOLIDAY PINE WREATH

Simple to construct and lovely to look at, this holiday wreath is brightened with gold metallic ribbons cascading through the design. PVC pine was chosen since the stems are wired and can be used to secure the ribbons and picks in the design. If you use a plastic or fresh pine wreath, simply add wire when attaching pieces (FIG. 7-5).
You will need:

- One 18-inch (45.5 cm) PVC pine wreath
- Seven 5-inch (12.5 cm) Christmas picks containing greens, a package, an apple, and berries
- 3¹/₂ yards (3 m) of 1¹/₂-inch-wide (4 cm) red plaid ribbon
- 4 yards (3.5 m) of 1¹/₂-inch-wide (4 cm) gold metallic ribbon
- 2 red chenille stems

1. Form a gold bow with eight 5-inch (12.5 cm) loops and no center loop. Form a plaid bow with eight 4-inch (10 cm) loops. Secure each with a chenille stem. Wire the gold bow to the top of the wreath and the plaid bow on top of the gold bow.

2. Cut stems of clusters to 3-inch (7.5 cm) lengths and insert all seven equally spaced around the wreath. When attaching, insert the pick into the wreath and wrap a piece of pine around the pick to secure.

Fig. 7-5
Christmas wreaths always make welcome gifts.

3. Hold 1¹/₂ yards (1.3 m) of the plaid ribbon on top of 1¹/₂ yards (1.3 m) of the gold ribbon and wire one end of each under one side of the bow.

4. Place the opposite ends together and wire under the other side of the bow.

5. In five locations around the wreath, pinch the two ribbons together and wrap a piece of pine around to keep in place.

PERSONAL TEDDY BEAR TREE

This design makes a lovely personal gift as it is perfect to fit on the corner of a table, desk, or window ledge (FIG. 7-6).
   You will need:

- One 12-inch (30.5 cm) × 8-inch (20 cm) wooden base
- 1 yard (.9 m) of 2¹/₂-inch-wide (6.5 cm) red velvet ribbon
- One 9-inch (22.5 cm) jointed teddy bear
- Two 3-inch (7.5 cm) × 2-inch (5 cm) gold wrapped packages with red ribbon bows

☐ One 12-inch (30.5 cm) miniature Christmas tree

☐ Five 2-inch (5 cm) flat felt Santa's

☐ Decorations of your choice for the tree—ours includes: 1 yard (9 m) gold chenille garland; twenty-four 1-inch (2.5 cm) wooden ornaments; twelve 2-inch (5 cm) candy canes; 2-inch (5 cm) chenille star for tree top

☐ White craft glue

1. Spread white craft glue over the wooden base and place three 12-inch (30.5 cm) lengths of ribbon side-by-side to cover.
2. Bend teddy bears legs and place in back right corner of the base. To permanently attach, glue to base.
3. Glue two packages in a stack in front of the bear.
4. Glue the tree to the back left corner of the base.
5. Attach the felt santas in a circle around the base of the tree.
6. Decorate the tree with your choice of decorations.

Fig. 7-6
This teddy bear tree will certainly brighten someone's Christmas.

The use of lace, pearls, and rosebuds in these designs reflect the romantic Victorian era. Some of the designs also incorporate potpourri, adding a pleasing aroma to any room.

These practical designs make great gifts for baby showers, housewarming parties, and birthdays.

Combining natural and artificial materials adds texture and visual interest to springtime designs.

The renewed feeling that comes with spring prompts us to brighten our homes with cheerful floral accents. Adding candy and cute stuffed animals will transform the designs into Easter baskets.

Although these displays look difficult to make, they were created using basic floral design principles that even beginners can master.

This versatile design is accented with dried and silk materials, creating a country theme.

Choose colors that complement each room's decor. The designs shown here add a welcoming touch to a guest room or bath.

Combining ordinary kitchen utensils such as a wooden spoon, rolling pin, and enamel kettle with dried materials give a countrified look to your kitchen decor. Choose colors that enhance your kitchen.

The use of woodsy materials and muted colors give these arrangements masculine appeal, making them perfect Father's Day gifts or den decorations.

The rich colors used in fall designs reflect the fiery display of nature. The Halloween arrangements shown here make attractive centerpieces and can be used to display treats that will delight the little tricksters in your house.

These designs are easy to make, using traditional Christmas colors and materials. Make several to give to friends and to decorate your own home during this festive holiday season.

CHAPTER 8

Gift
Baskets

*U*nique gift baskets can be created that will please and delight both the giver and the receiver of the basket. Keep in mind that you can change and adapt the suggestions given here to design a basket that will perfectly match the personality of the recipient.

NURSERY TEDDY BEAR BAG

Not all gift baskets need to be "baskets." Here a gift bag is designed to hold a teddy bear for the newborn and flowers for mom (FIG. 8-1).

You will need:

☐ Teddy bear of your choice
☐ Gift bag sized to comfortably hold the chosen teddy bear
☐ Sheets of colored tissue to coordinate with the colors of the bag
☐ Silk flowers to coordinated with the colors of the bag. We used: three 2-inch (5 cm) pink rosebuds, 1 stem baby blue double blossoms, and 1-ounce package bleached sparkle gypsophila
☐ 28-gauge wire
☐ Green floral tape

1. Insert the bear into the bag. You want his head to extend above the bag. If he falls too low in the bag, place stuffing or balls of tissue under the bear to raise it higher.
2. Cut 12-inch (30.5 cm) squares of tissue in assorted colors. Pinch together one end of the tissue and insert the pinched end into the bag between the bear and the bag. Place a number of color sheets surrounding the bear.
3. Hold the flowers all together in a group, breaking the glittered gyp into smaller pieces to distribute throughout. Wrap the wire snugly around the floral cluster and wrap over the wire with floral tape.

Fig. 8-1 (Above Left)
Not all "gift baskets" are
baskets.

Fig. 8-2 (Above Right)
Towel and soap gift baskets
are perfect hostess gifts.

4. Insert the floral cluster into the bag between the bear's hands so it appears as though he is holding it.

SOAP & TOWEL GIFT BASKET

This wonderful gift basket was actually a gift to me from a dear friend, Barb Hils of Cincinnati, OH. I enjoyed receiving it so much that I wanted to share it with you (FIG. 8-2). Coordinate the colors with the room of the recipient.

You will need:

☐ Duck design wicker basket

☐ Three to four decorative towels and washcloths

☐ Package of soaps to coordinate with the towels

☐ Sheet of tissue paper

☐ One stem starburst flowers

☐ One stem double blossom flowers

☐ Small bunch gypsophila

☐ 1¹/₂ yards (1.3 m) of 1-inch-wide (2.5 cm) lace edge ribbon

☐ 28-gauge wire

☐ Green floral tape

☐ 1 chenille stem

1. Lay tissue paper into basket with more tissue extending out the back of the basket.

2. Roll towels and washcloths and insert into basket. Place soap in front of the towels.
3. Form a bow with the ribbon having 6-inch (15 cm) streamers and eight 2-inch (5 cm) loops. Secure with a chenille stem.
4. Lay 8-inch (20 cm) lengths of all the floral materials together in a cluster with the gypsophila interspersed throughout the silks. Wire in a cluster and floral tape over the wired spot.
5. Attach the bow to the front of the cluster. Trim the chenille stem ends and insert the cluster into the basket.

ROMANTIC BALLOON GIFT BASKET

A quick basket design can be created when a last-minute gift is needed (FIG. 8-3). When creating this design, first choose the gift items that will go into the basket. Then select a basket that will comfortably hold and adequately display these items.

You will need:

☐ Gift items of your choice

☐ Basket of your choice

☐ Two helium-filled latex balloons on ribbons

☐ Iridescent shredded grass

☐ Two satin flowers to coordinate with the basket color

1. Fill basket with shredded grass and lay items in a pleasing arrangement into the basket.
2. Tie balloons to handle of basket so that one balloon is higher than the other.
3. Remove the flower heads from their stems and lay into the basket.

HAPPY BIRTHDAY BALLOON BASKET

Birthdays are festive and fun. Create a gift basket to represent this festive spirit (FIG. 8-4).

You will need:

☐ One 11-inch-wide (28 cm) × 12-inch-tall (30.5 cm) wicker basket

☐ Three helium-filled latex balloons on ribbons

☐ One stem yellow mums containing three flowers with 2-inch- (5 cm), 3-inch- (7.5 cm), and 4-inch-wide (10 cm) heads

☐ Two red carnations with 3-inch-wide (7.5 cm) heads

☐ One party hat

☐ One Lomey caged Sahara foam

☐ Two 12-inch (30.5 cm) sheets blue glossy paper

Fig. 8-3
Preparation of this romantic gift basket took less than 15 minutes.

Fig. 8-4 (Above Left)
Birthday gift baskets can be
great fun.

Fig. 8-5 (Above Right)
Tie three helium-filled latex
balloons to the left handle
of the basket.

☐ Two 12-inch (30.5 cm) sheets red glossy paper
☐ Stapler
☐ Hot-glue gun and sticks

1. Tie the three latex balloons to the left handle of the basket so that the balloons are at various heights (FIG. 8-5).
2. Pinch the ends of each blue and red sheet of paper together and staple to resemble a fan shape .
3. Form a vertical design in the Lomey caged foam. See chapter 6 for basic vertical instructions. Glue the foam into the right side of the basket to get the proper flower heights before inserting flowers.
4. The mum bud should extend above the basket handle. The carnations and other two mums should alternate down to the basket rim.
5. Insert the fan shapes of paper around the balloons and in the back of the basket.
6. Place the birthday hat into the basket between the balloons and flowers.

Romantic Designs

*R*omantic gifts are always appreciated. Their soft delicate appearance is pleasing. We've used potpourri in several of the designs to add the extra special touch a pleasing fragrance provides.

POTPOURRI HEART

This lovely design is easy to make and would be appreciated by moms, grandmas, teachers, and friends (FIG. 9-1).

You will need:

☐ 8-inch (20 cm) Styrofoam heart and 3-ounce bag rose potpourri

—OR—

☐ 8-inch (20 cm) prepared potpourri heart

☐ Three mauve rosebuds with 1¹/₂-inch-wide (4 cm) heads

☐ Six stems purple statice sinuata

☐ 2 yards (1.8 m) of ¹/₂-inch-wide (1.3 cm) eggshell lace ribbon

☐ ¹/₂ yard (45.5 cm) of ¹/₄-inch-wide (.5 cm) blue picot-edge ribbon

☐ White craft glue

1. If the heart you purchase is not already covered with potpourri, spread it with white glue, and roll in potpourri until completely covered. Let dry.
2. Remove the heads of the rosebuds and glue in a cluster at the lower right corner of the heart.
3. Break off statice heads and glue around the rosebuds.
4. Cut four 3-inch (7.5 cm) lengths of lace ribbon. Bring ends together to form a loop and glue all four between the roses and statice.
5. Cut three lace streamers and two picot streamers from the remaining ribbon with each being slightly different lengths than the others.
6. Bring all the ends together and glue under the head of the bottom rosebud.

DECORATIVE POTPOURRI DISH

The design of the Lomey dish is perfect to display potpourri and allow it to become a decorative accent as well as the enjoyment of its aroma (FIG. 9-2).

You will need:

☐ One Series 48 or 49 Lomey dish—8½-inch-wide (21.5 cm) dish-type container

☐ One mauve open rose with 4-inch-wide (10 cm) head

☐ Three celedon green flowers with 2-inch (5 cm) heads

☐ One mauve trumpet flower with 2-inch (5 cm) head

☐ Three stems mauve floral buds

☐ Twelve circular pearl stems with 2-inch (5 cm) loops

☐ Twelve shooting pearl stems

☐ 3 yards (2.5 m) of ½-inch-wide (1.3 cm) mauve picot edge ribbon

☐ 3 yards (2.5 m) of ¼-inch (.5 cm) celedon green picot edge ribbon

☐ 3 yards (2.5 m) of ¼-inch (.5 cm) purple edge sheer ribbon

☐ 28-gauge cloth-covered wire

☐ 3-ounce package home decor potpourri

☐ Green floral tape

☐ Hot-glue gun and glue sticks

1. Fill the Lomey dish with potpourri.
2. Create a floral cluster with the flowers and pearls. All will be floral-taped together. Begin at the tip with one stem of floral buds and hold a shooting pearl and circular pearl stem together and floral-tape.
3. Next add the trumpet flower 2 inches (5 cm) below the top of the buds and tape in place.
4. Add one celedon flower below the trumpet flower and angled to the right, as well as one angled to the left 1/2 inch (1.3 cm) lower than the first. Floral-tape in place.
5. Floral-tape one floral bud stem below and to the right. Place five shooting and five circular pearl stems around and through these last flowers and floral-tape in place.
6. Place the open flower below the flowers already in place and floral-tape together. Add the remaining celedon green flower and all pearls below the open rose and tape all together. Trim the stem ends. Glue this cluster to the left side of the bowl.
7. Form a bow with each of the ribbons having 12-inch (30.5 cm) streamers and eight 2-inch (5 cm) loops. Secure with wire and wire all in a bunch under the floral cluster. Glue remaining ribbon cut into 10-inch (25.5 cm) to 12-inch (30.5 cm) streamers under the bow. Twist and curl all streamers separately and glue to the container edge as shown in FIG. 9-2.

EVERLASTING HEART

The dried flowers used in this lovely heart-shaped form are accented with tiny ribbons to create interest and contrast (FIG. 9-3).

You will need:

☐ One Lomey eggshell Sweetheart Bouquet holder with Sahara foam

☐ One bunch Holland dried roses (approx. 22 roses)

☐ 1-ounce bunch white statice sinuata

☐ 5 yards (4.5 m) of 1/8-inch-wide (.2 cm) burgundy double-face satin ribbon

☐ Wired wood picks

☐ Hot-glue gun and sticks, or white craft glue

1. Break the white statice into pieces with approximately 1 1/2-inch (4 cm) long stems. Insert throughout foam repeating heart shape of lace collar.
2. Cut the stems of the roses to 2 inches (5 cm) and insert throughout the statice staying within the heart shape established with the statice.
3. Cut six 1/2-yard (.5 m) pieces of ribbon. Form a four loop pick with each securing to a wood pick.

Fig. 9-3 (Above Left)
The dried flowers used in a lovely heart-shaped holder are accented with tiny ribbons to create interest and contrast.

Fig. 9-4 (Above Right)
The concept of the gathering basket is popular in home decorating.

4. Form a bow with remaining 2 yards (1.8 m) having eight 2-inch (5 cm) loops and three 12-inch (30.5 cm) streamers. Secure this to a wood pick and tie overhand knots in streamer ends.
5. Insert the bow at the heart point and the remaining loops throughout the design.

GATHERING BASKET

A gathering basket was commonly used by ladies to carry into the garden to pick flowers that were at their prime. In our version, the basket is decorated first; you may fill the basket with your choice of materials (FIG. 9-4).

You will need:

☐ One 10-inch (25.5 cm) × 8-inch (20 cm) open flaired basket

☐ 1½ yard (1.3 m) mauve whitewashed untwisted paper ribbon

☐ 1¼-ounce preserved green Candy Tuff

☐ Two Holland dried rose heads

☐ Approximately 18 mauve dried Florentine heads

☐ Cloth-covered wire

☐ Hot-glue gun and sticks, or white craft glue

1. First untwist the paper ribbon and slit it in half lengthwise. Cut a 24-inch (70 cm) length of ribbon and wrap it around the base of the basket, securing with cloth-covered wire and glueing at the handle.
2. Form a bow with 1¹/₂ yards (1.3 m) ribbon, leaving streamers 12 inches (30.5 cm) long. Attach the bow to the base of the handle with the wire, securing it.
3. Pinch and glue one of the streamers along the top of the handle and the other along the rim of the basket.
4. Break the Candy Tuff into 1-inch (2.5 cm) to 3-inch (7.5 cm) lengths and glue into the bow loops with tiny pieces along the pinched portions of ribbon.
5. Glue one rose head at each pinched ribbon portion, with the remainder throughout the bow loops. Cut the stems off of the Florentine flowers and glue three heads around each rose on the pinched ribbon and the others throughout the bow loops and flowers.

MOTHER'S DAY HEART DESIGN

Beautiful floral gifts for mom are always enjoyed and appreciated. This design has a romantic Victorian feel, yet ties into the natural look of wicker (FIG. 9-5).

You will need:

- [ ] One 10-inch-wide (25.5 cm) × 1¹/₂-inch-tall (4 cm) white Styrofoam disk
- [ ] 1 yard (.9 m) of 1¹/₂-inch-wide (4 cm) mauve moiré ribbon
- [ ] 1-ounce package green Spanish moss
- [ ] One 9-inch-wide (22.5 cm) × 2¹/₂-inch-deep (6.5 cm) woven heart basket
- [ ] One 4-inch-wide (10 cm) × 2¹/₂-inch-deep (6.5 cm) woven heart basket
- [ ] 2 yards (1.8 m) of 1¹/₂-inch-wide eggshell and mauve lace ribbon
- [ ] 2 yards (1.8 m) of 6-inch-wide (15 cm) eggshell tulle
- [ ] Nine 2-inch (5 cm) mauve china silk roses
- [ ] Three 4-inch (10 cm) eggshell satin lily of the valley stems with five lily sections per stem
- [ ] Four 8-inch (20 cm) mauve berry stems
- [ ] Cloth-covered wire
- [ ] Straight pins
- [ ] U-shaped craft pins
- [ ] White craft glue, hot-glue gun and sticks

Fig. 9-5
Beautiful floral gifts for mom are always
enjoyed and appreciated.

1. Wrap the disk with moiré ribbon and pin the ends to secure. Spread the Spanish moss over the disk and secure with U-shaped craft pins.

2. Using craft pins and glue, secure the larger heart to the back of the disk angled slightly to the left and the smaller heart to the front of the disk angled slightly to the right.

3. Form a bow with the lace ribbon having 18-inch (45.5 cm) streamers and six 3-inch (7.5 cm) loops. Repeat with the tulle. Secure the lace bow on top of the tulle bow with cloth-covered wire and trim away excess wire. Pin this double bow onto the foam between the hearts. The streamers will be placed throughout the flowers later.

4. Refer to the basic instructions for the S-curve design in chapter 5 to help you construct this piece. First use the roses to form an S shape, extending from the top of the larger basket to the front of the smaller basket. The stems will be cut longer for the outer flowers and shorter for the central flowers.

5. Cut the stems of the three lily of the valley stems to 2 inches (5 cm) and insert the three equally spaced down the center of the design.

6. Cut the stems of the berry sprays to 2-inch (5 cm) lengths and insert one on the upper portion of the S, one on the lower portion, and one on either side of the center.

7. Weave the streamers through the flowers on the upper and lower portion of the S and wrap with cloth-covered wire to the ends of the flowers in the design.

Spring Designs

*T*he fresh clean feeling of spring fills us with a feeling of excitement. We wish to spruce up our homes indoors and out and add special floral designs to brighten up our walls and tables.

WHITEWASHED PALM WREATH

The whitewashed look is becoming increasingly popular. Here it is combined with spring birds and berry branches. See FIG. 10-1 on p. 100.

You will need:

☐ One 18-inch (45.5 cm) whitewashed grapevine wreath

☐ One 6-inch (15 cm) piece ming moss

☐ Five blue palm spears approx. 6 inches (15 cm) long

☐ 2¹/₂ yards (2.3 m) of 1-inch-wide (2.5 cm) mauve gauze-like ribbon

☐ 3 yards (2.5 m) of 1¹/₂-inch-wide (4 cm) blue gauze-like ribbon

☐ One 3-inch (7.5 cm) nest

☐ Four 18-inch (45.5 cm) mauve berry branches

☐ One 4-inch (10 cm) blue partridge

☐ One 2-inch (5 cm) blue partridge

☐ Four 1-inch (2.5 cm) bird eggs

☐ Four mauve-burgundy straw flowers approx. 2 inches (5 cm) wide

☐ One eggshell chenille stem

☐ 28-gauge cloth-covered wire

☐ Hot-glue gun and sticks

☐ X-ACTO® knife

1. Begin by breaking the ming moss into smaller pieces and glueing them at the base of the wreath in a grouping.
2. Cut the stem of one small palm at an angle to a 5-inch (12.5 cm) length. Insert into the center of the wreath behind the moss. Cut the stem of a

second palm to 3 inches (7.5 cm) and insert into the front right corner

3. Cut three more palms to 3-inch (7.5 cm) stem lengths. Glue one below and to the right of the bottom palm, the second angled into the left side of the moss, and the last angled into the upper right corner.

4. Form a bow with eight 4-inch (10 cm) loops, two 18-inch (45.5 cm) streamers, and no center loop from one of the gauze-like ribbons. Repeat with the other ribbon, forming it with 3-inch (7.5 cm) loops, two 18-inch (45.5 cm) streamers, and no center loop. Secure each bow with cloth-covered wire. Place the second bow on top of the first and wire the two together. Glue this double bow onto the moss near the center of the palms.

5. Glue the nest into the center of the bow.

6. Cut four 12-inch (30.5 cm) lengths of mauve berry branch. These four should be inserted straight up into the left side of the wreath. Cut four 6-inch (15 cm) lengths of the berries, and glue closer to the base.

Fig. 10-1 (Below Left) Berries and whitewashed pods are lovely spring accents.

7. Curl the streamers of the ribbon, and glue up the left side of the wreath. Glue the 4-inch (10 cm) partridge to the left side of the nest and the 2-inch (5 cm) partridge to the right side of the nest.

Fig. 10-2 (Below Right) Dried flower heads are the perfect accent for this paper-maché bunny design.

8. Using the X-ACTO knife, cut one of the eggs open in a jagged fashion and glue it inside the nest. Glue the remaining two eggs in the nest.

9. Cut the stems of four straw flowers to 2 inches (5 cm) and glue two of them to the lower right side of the nest. Glue the second two flowers to the left side of the nest.

SPRING MÂCHÉ BUNNY

Florals are used in a new way to decorate the form of a paper-mâché bunny complete with a tiny Easter basket (FIG. 10-2).

You will need:

☐ One 11-inch-tall (28 cm) paper-mâché bunny form

☐ 6-ounce bag dried baby's breath

☐ 1-inch (2.5 cm) pink chenille stem

☐ Two pieces purple statice sinuata

☐ Two ¹/₂-inch (1.3 m) premade ribbon roses

☐ 1 yard (.9 m) of ¹/₈-inch-wide (.2 cm) pink double-face satin ribbon

☐ 1 yard (.9 m) of ¹/₈-inch-wide (.2 cm) yellow double-face satin ribbon

☐ 1 yard (.9 m) of ¹/₈-inch-wide (.2 cm) purple double-face satin ribbon

☐ Cotton ball

☐ Eggshell acrylic paint

☐ 1-inch (2.5 cm) sponge brush

☐ Easter basket and jelly bean eggs

☐ White craft glue

1. Paint the entire mâché form with eggshell paint.
2. When dry, spread portions with white craft glue. While still wet, place baby's breath heads which have been broken from main stems onto glue and let dry. (*Note*: Dried baby's breath is very brittle. Simply roll stems in your hands and they will fall apart and be in perfect shape to use to cover bunny.)
3. When completely covered, return and glue pieces of baby's breath with 1-inch (2.5 cm) stems in the area of the ears to create dimension.
4. Glue the chenille stem curled into a circle as the bunny's nose and the two statice pieces as his eyes.
5. Form a 6-inch (15 cm) braid with the three satin ribbons and glue around the mâché form from ear to ear. Form a bow, using all three ribbons, and glue to the neck near the eye.
6. Glue one rose in the bow center and one to the front of the neck.

SPRING FRIENDLY BASKET

This perky spring design is simple to create and will add friendly cheer wherever it is used (FIG. 10-3).

You will need:

☐ One 8-inch-wide (20 cm) × 4-inch-tall (10 cm) basket with 14-inch-tall (35 cm) handle

☐ ¹/₂ block Sahara II foam

☐ 1-ounce package Spanish moss

☐ Eight 8-inch (20 cm) ivy sprigs

☐ Eleven 5-inch (12.5 cm) daisy stems with two 2-inch (5 cm) white daisies per stem

☐ Sixteen 6-inch pink alstroemeria stems with two 2-inch (5 cm) open flowers and one bud per stem

☐ Four 8-inch (20 cm) purple freesia

☐ Hot-glue gun and sticks

☐ U-shaped craft pins

☐ Wired wooden picks

1. Glue the foam into the basket and cover with moss, securing with U-shaped craft pins.

2. Refer to the mound design basics in chapter 4 as you create this design. The daisy stems will be your main flowers: insert six in the first row, four in the second, and one in the center.

3. Insert six alstroemeria in the first row between the daisies. Insert a second row of six flowers in a row of their own. Insert four in a row between the daisies.

4. Insert the four freesia throughout the center of the design.

Fig. 10-3 (Below Left)
This perky spring design is easy to create and will add friendly cheer to its recipient.

Fig. 10-4 (Below Right)
This natural-looking design is perfect for your spring table.

5. Glue two ivy sprigs end to end along one side of the handle. Cut the remaining sprigs to 4-inch (10 cm) lengths and insert throughout the design. If necessary, attach these to wood picks before insertion.

NATURE'S BEAUTY

The natural look of this design makes it a perfect accent for a table this spring (FIG. 10-4).

You will need:

☐ One Lomey 8¹/₂-inch (21 cm) Series 49 container
☐ One 3¹/₂-inch (8.5 cm) grey excelsior nest
☐ Six pieces of baby red eucalyptus
☐ 8 straw flowers
☐ One 4-inch (10 cm) partridge
☐ 1-ounce package white branches approx. 12 inches (30.5 cm) long
☐ 1-ounce package blue statice sinuata
☐ 1-ounce package preserved sprengerii fern
☐ 2¹/₂-inch (6.5 cm) × 3-inch (7.5 cm) × 2-inch (5 cm) block Sahara II foam
☐ 1-ounce package Spanish moss
☐ U-shaped craft pins
☐ White craft glue, and hot-glue gun and sticks

1. Glue the foam into the container, cover with moss, and secure with U-shaped craft pins. Let moss extend gently over container edges.
2. Insert one 17-inch (43 cm), two 12-inch (30.5 cm), one 10-inch (25.5 cm), one 8-inch (20 cm), and one 6-inch (15 cm) stems of eucalyptus into the back and sides of the container, arranging in a fan shape.
3. Glue the nest and bird to the right front edge of the container.
4. Cut stems of straw flowers and insert three above the nest and the remaining five around base of container.
5. Break the branches into shorter pieces and insert throughout the eucalyptus and straw flowers.
6. Break stems of static and sprengerii to 1-inch (2.5 cm) to 3-inch (7.5 cm) lengths and insert throughout the design to fill any extra space.

Kitchen Designs

*T*he kitchen is where we all meet and many fond memories are made. Many times, we spend more time in the kitchen than we do in any other room in the house. Gifts created for the kitchen are very special.

KITCHEN KETTLE MOUND DESIGN

This design suggests the gathering of flowers and their simple insertion into a lovely kettle, reminiscent of long-ago days (FIG. 11-1).

You will need:

- [ ] One 6-inch-wide (15 cm) × 5-inch-tall (12.5 cm) blue enamel pot with lid
- [ ] One block of Sahara II foam
- [ ] Five stems of white silk starburst flowers—each containing four sections of six flowers each
- [ ] Five stems of yellow silk starburst flowers—each containing four sections of six flowers each
- [ ] 1-ounce package excelsior
- [ ] U-shaped craft pins
- [ ] Hot-glue gun and sticks

1. Glue the Sahara II to the bottom of the pot. Cover with excelsior and secure with U-shaped pins.
2. Follow the instructions in chapter 4 for the casual mass style of arranging. Cut the stems of the starburst and insert throughout the foam to resemble FIG. 11-2 in roundness and fullness.
3. Glue the lid next to the pot.

KITCHEN WALL BASKET

The dried materials in this design give it a country look. Adapt the colors to coordinate with your kitchen (FIG. 11-3).

You will need:

- [ ] One 4-inch-wide (10 cm) × 5-inch-tall (12.5 cm) wall basket
- [ ] ¹/₂ block of Sahara II foam
- [ ] One 2-ounce bunch of preserved gypsophila
- [ ] Two stems of yellow silk daisies—each stem containing three sprigs of two 2-inch (5 cm) flowers
- [ ] Two stems of blue silk double blossom flowers—each stem containing six sprigs of flowers
- [ ] 2 yards (1.8 m) of ¹/₂-inch-wide (1.3 cm) blue heart patterned ribbon
- [ ] One 5-inch (12.5 cm) wooden rolling pin
- [ ] One 5-inch (12.5 cm) wire whip
- [ ] One 5-inch (12.5 cm) wooden mallet
- [ ] One 4-inch (10 cm) wooden words "kitchen"
- [ ] 1-ounce package excelsior
- [ ] Hot-glue gun and sticks
- [ ] U-shaped craft pins
- [ ] Cloth-covered wire
- [ ] Wired wood picks

1. Glue the foam to the bottom of the container, cover with excelsior, and secure with U-shaped craft pins.

Fig. 11-1 (Above Left)
A kettle is wonderful for a kitchen-style arrangement.

Fig. 11-2 (Above Right)
Tiny kitchen utensils accent this design.

2. Follow the instructions in chapter 4 for the casual mass style of design to assist you in completing this design. Break all gypsophila into lengths of 6 inches (15 cm) to 8 inches (20 cm), and insert into the foam to form a rounded shape.
3. Cut stems of daisies to same lengths and insert throughout gypsophila.
4. Form a ten-loop bow with 2¹/₂-inch (6.5 cm) loops and 6-inch (15 cm) streamers, secure with wire, and insert into foam in the front left side . of the design.
5. Glue "kitchen" to front of basket. Attach wood picks to ends of kitchen items and insert all in a group to the right of bow.

KITCHEN SPOON

This design is quick and easy to make. The wooden spoon is easy to find, simply choose colors that coordinate with your kitchen (FIG. 11-3).

   You will need:

☐ One 12-inch (30.5 cm) wooden spoon

☐ Four sprigs of silk flowers in assorted colors to coordinate with room

☐ One sprig preserved baby's breath

☐ ¹/₂ yard (45.5 cm) of ¹/₄-inch-wide (.6 cm) red heart ribbon

☐ Hot-glue gun and sticks

☐ Cloth-covered wire

Fig. 11-3
An embellished wooden spoon will add a special touch to any location in your kitchen.

1. Form a four-loop bow with 2-inch (5 cm) loops and 5-inch (12.5 cm) streamers, securing with cloth-covered wire.
2. Glue the bow to the top of the spoon. Break the baby's breath and silks, cut the stems short, and glue through the bow loops.

CHAPTER 12

Fall
Designs

The sights and scents of fall make it one of my favorite times of the year. Rich colors are one of the traditional trademarks and are therefore represented in this collection of designs.

FALL CORNUCOPIA

Cornucopias are popular design elements for fall and Halloween. Simple to create, they add a lovely touch to our holiday tables (FIG. 12-1).
    You will need:

☐ One 12-inch (30.5 cm) cornucopia basket

☐ One 2-ounce bunch preserved fall oak leaves

☐ Seven yellow carnations, each with a 2-inch (5 cm) head

☐ Three orange lacquered pumpkins, each with a 3-inch (7.5 cm) head

☐ One 1-ounce bunch preserved baby's breath

☐ ½ block Sahara II foam

☐ 1-ounce bag excelsior

☐ U-shaped craft pins

☐ Hot-glue gun and sticks

1. Glue Sahara II to the inside of the cornucopia. Cover it with excelsior and secure with U-shaped craft pins.
2. Cut stems of leaves to 3-inch (7.5 cm) lengths and insert in a circle around the edge of the cornucopia.
3. Cut stems of pumpkins to 3-inch (7.5 cm) lengths and insert in a group in the center of the foam. Surround the pumpkins with carnations, which have had their stems cut to 4 inches (10 cm).
4. Break gypsophila and more leaf stems to 4 inches (10 cm) and insert throughout flowers and pumpkins.

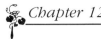

Fig. 12-1 (Above Left)
Cornucopias are popular
design elements for fall.

Fig. 12-2 (Above Right)
Your little tricksters will like
this table design.

SPOOKY OL'TREE CENTERPIECE

This delightful design is easy to create and can display your Halloween
candy for the little "tricksters" in your house (FIG. 12-2).
    You will need:

☐ One 16-inch (40.5 cm) wicker mat

☐ 1¹/₂ yards (1.3 m) of 1¹/₂-inch-wide (4 cm) orange Halloween ribbon

☐ 1-ounce package Spanish moss

☐ One 14-inch-tall (35 cm) wooden tree centerpiece on base

☐ 6 yards (5.5 m) of ⁷/₈-inch-wide (2.2 cm) black Halloween ribbon

☐ Eighteen 1-inch (2.5 cm) lacquered pumpkins

☐ Four ³/₄-inch-wide (2 cm) wide flocked pumpkins

☐ Three 3-inch-tall (7.5 cm) ghosts

☐ Six stems yellow silk mums with 3-inch (7.5 cm) heads

☐ Six stems rust silk mums with 3-inch (7.5 cm) heads

☐ Eighteen 2-inch (5 cm) yellow silk fall leaves

☐ Trick or treat candy bars

☐ Cloth-covered wire

1. Weave the 1¹/₂-inch-wide (4 cm) ribbon around the edges of the mat.
   Glue the tree into the center of the mat, cover the base with Spanish
   moss, and glue in place.

2. Form an eight-loop bow with 2-inch (5 cm) loops and no center loop from the black Halloween ribbon. Form six bows in all. Glue these equally spaced around the base of the mat. Glue three 1-inch (2.5 cm) lacquered pumpkins in the center of each bow.
3. Glue four flocked pumpkins and three ghosts to the tree branches.
4. Pull the heads off of the mums and glue all around the base of the tree in the moss. Glue three leaves in a cluster between each bow.
5. Place trick or treat candy around the base of the design.

SCARECROW ARRANGEMENT

This cute design is useful for fall or Halloween. A tall mound styling is used for construction (FIG. 12-3).

You will need:

- One 14-inch (35 cm) flat walnut base
- 3-inch (7.5 cm) square block Sahara II foam
- 1-ounce package Spanish moss
- One 8-inch-tall (20 cm) scarecrow and haystack figurine
- Five stems orange lilies with two groups of three 2-inch (5 cm) flowers and one bud per stem
- Two stems rust azaleas with two groups of three 2-inch (5 cm) flowers per stem
- Two stems brown double blossoms with six sprigs per stem
- Two stems yellow-orange leaves with four leaf sections per stem
- One 2½-inch lacquered pumpkin
- Two 1½-inch lacquered pumpkins
- Hot-glue gun and sticks
- U-shaped craft pins

1. Glue the foam to the left side of the walnut base, cover with moss, and secure with U-shaped pins.
2. Glue scarecrow figurine to right side of base, with three pumpkins glued in front of figurine.
3. Cut one group of lilies to 15-inch (38 cm) stem length and insert into the center of the foam. Cut five sections to 7-inch (17.5 cm) stem lengths and insert equally spaced around base of design. Cut remaining four sections to 11 inches (28 cm) and insert at an angle into the foam equally spaced around in a row between top flower and base flowers.
4. Cut the stems of brown double blossom flowers apart and insert randomly throughout the design to fill space.
5. Cut sections of silk leaves apart and insert four sections around the base and four more sections in the center of the design.

Fig. 12-3 (Above Left)
Fall is nicely depicted in the colors of this scarecrow arrangement.

Fig. 12-4 (Above Right)
Old and young people alike will love this Halloween display for candy.

TRICK OR TREAT DISPLAY

This is a wonderful idea when creating a design for a table display or perhaps for the entryway of an office building. The candy is easily accessible and displayed in an attractive manner (FIG. 12-4).

You will need:

☐ One 18-inch (45.5 cm) × 12-inch (30.5 cm) × 2-inch (5 cm) Styrofoam sheet

☐ One 5-inch (12.5 cm) × 5-inch (12.5 cm) × 3-inch (7.5 cm) Styrofoam block

☐ One 4-inch (10 cm) × 2-inch (5 cm) × 3-inch (7.5 cm) Styrofoam block covered with a 12-inch (30.5 cm) length of tan paper ribbon

☐ One 4-inch (10 cm) × 3-inch (7.5 cm) × 1-inch (2.5 cm) Styrofoam block

☐ One block Sahara II foam

☐ One 9-inch (22.5 cm) × 10-inch (25.5 cm) basket

☐ One 5-inch (12.5 cm) × 8-inch (20 cm) basket

☐ One 7-inch (17.5 cm) × 10-inch (25.5 cm) basket

☐ One set of three nested Halloween tins with lids, largest tin should be 4 inches (10 cm) tall × 4 inches (10 cm) wide

☐ 6-ounce package natural gypsy grass

☐ Two fall floral bushes—each bush containing eight to ten 3-inch (7.5 cm) flowers

☐ Two large bags green Spanish moss

☐ One bunch natural branches; the branches should vary in lengths between 12 inches (30.5 cm) to 24 inches (70 cm)

☐ U-shaped craft pins

☐ White craft glue

1. Following the diagram in FIG. 12-5, glue Sahara and Styrofoam pieces to large base. When dry, pin Spanish moss over entire design.
2. Following the casual mass basics in chapter 4, form a design in the Sahara foam on the left using the gypsy grass, and cutting the bushes into separate flowers and inserting throughout. Insert the branches as shown in FIG. 12-4.
3. Place the baskets and tins in place in the design and fill with candy. The baskets can be pinned to the foam if desired. The tins can be glued if desired.

Fig. 12-5 (Left)
Overhead diagram of placement of materials for the Halloween display.

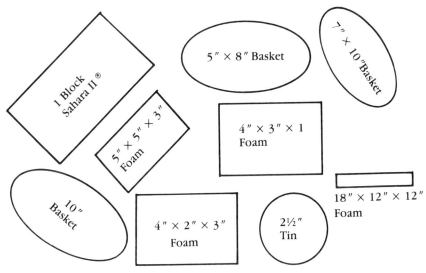

Base of Design - Construction of foam pieces

CHAPTER 13

Home Decor

*D*ecorating our homes or those of our friends or loved ones with floral designs is very rewarding. Several designs are explained here, each having its own unique form and appeal. Choose colors and flower styles that will complement the colors and decor of your room.

TOPIARY TREE

The topiary tree was especially popular in Victorian times. Although its appeal cooled for many years, it is back stronger than ever (FIG. 13-1).

You will need:

- [ ] One 4-inch-wide (10 cm) × 3-inch-tall (7.5 cm) wicker basket
- [ ] One 6-inch (15 cm) Styrofoam ball
- [ ] 12-inch (30.5 cm) length of ¹/₂-inch-wide (1.3 cm) dowel rod
- [ ] Five picks containing blue apples, packages, and berries
- [ ] Twenty-four gold glittered cedar picks approx. 4 inches (10 cm) wide
- [ ] 6¹/₂ yards (6 m) of 1¹/₂-inch-wide (4 cm) peach/eggshell lace ribbon
- [ ] 6¹/₂ yards (6 m) of ³/₄-inch-wide (2 cm) peach satin ribbon
- [ ] 6¹/₂ yards (6 m) of 1¹/₂-inch-wide (4 cm) blue moiré ribbon
- [ ] ¹/₂ block Sahara II
- [ ] U-shaped craft pins
- [ ] 1-ounce package Spanish moss
- [ ] Hot-glue gun and sticks, white craft glue
- [ ] Twelve eggshell chenille stems

1. Glue foam block inside basket. Cover foam with moss and secure with U-shaped craft pins. Insert end of dowel into glue and then insert into center of foam.
2. Add glue to other end of dowel and insert halfway into 6-inch (15 cm) ball.
3. Cut 10 lengths of lace ribbon 18 inches (45.5 cm) long. Repeat with peach satin ribbon and blue moiré ribbon. Cut chenille stems in half.

4. Form three 3-inch (7.5 cm) loops from the blue moiré. Wrap a chenille stem around the base of the three loops, and twist the ends together all the way to the ends. Repeat to form all 10 loop picks with blue moiré.

5. Place the peach satin on top of the lace and form the same type of pick as described in step 4. Repeat to form all 10 picks.

6. Cut stems of package picks and cedar stems to 2-inch (5 cm) lengths and insert these, plus ribbon loops, equally spaced around ball to completely cover. Use U-shaped craft pins to help secure ribbons.

7. Wrap the dowel rod in one direction with blue moiré ribbon and in opposite direction with peach satin. Glue ends to secure.

8. Form two bows with blue moiré ribbon, each having four 2-inch (5 cm) loops, and secure with chenille stems. Repeat with lace ribbon having loops 3 inches (7.5 cm) long. Wire blue bow on top of lace bow and insert one bow on either side of the dowel rod at the tree base.

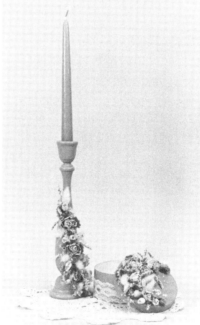

Fig. 13-1 (Left)
Topiary trees are making a big comeback.

Fig. 13-2 (Right)
Made to coordinate, these pieces will add a romantic touch to your home.

POTPOURRI BOX & CANDLESTICK

Made to coordinate together, these pieces will add a romantic touch to your home, as well as a wonderful aroma to the room (FIG. 13-2).

You will need:

☐ One 12-inch (30.5 cm) wooden candlestick

☐ One 4-inch (10 cm) round chipboard box

☐ One bunch of mauve lagurus (bunny tails) with at least 16 stems

☐ One bunch natural dried yellow rosebuds with at least 9 stems

☐ One bunch purple statice with at least 12 stems to the bunch

☐ One small bunch German statice

☐ One bunch pink Florentine dried flowers with at least 12 stems

☐ 12 inches (30.5 cm) of 1¹/₂-inch-wide (4 cm) eggshell and mauve lace ribbon

☐ Mauve acrylic paint

☐ Sponge brush

☐ Hot-glue gun and sticks, white craft glue

☐ Potpourri to fill box

☐ Candle to insert into holder

1. Paint candlestick, box, and lid. When dry, glue lace ribbon around base of bottom of box.
2. Break off the stems of the following flowers and glue them in a crescent design around the lid of the box: five rosebuds, six lagurus, seven Florentine flowers, five purple statice, and several small pieces of German statice.
3. Glue remaining heads of flowers down the front of the candlestick.
4. Fill box with potpourri of your choice.

STATICE CAT

This unique use of statice adds a lovely romantic touch to any room (FIG. 13-3).

You will need:

☐ One paper-mâché cat form approx. 12 inches (30.5 cm) across

☐ Three 4-ounce bunches of purple statice

☐ Three 1-inch (2.5 cm) white ribbon roses

☐ One 1-inch (2.5 cm) purple ribbon rose

☐ 6-inch (15 cm) length 2 mm fused pearls

☐ 1 yard (.9 m) of 1¹/₂-inch-wide (4 cm) iridescent lace ribbon

☐ ¹/₂ yard (.5 m) of ¹/₂-inch-wide (1.3 cm) iridescent lace ribbon

☐ Purple acrylic paint

☐ Sponge brush

☐ Hot-glue gun and sticks, white craft glue

1. Paint entire cat form purple, let dry.
2. Break off the heads of the statice and glue close together, completely covering cat form.

3. Cut 1-inch (2.5 cm) lengths of pearls, and glue in curved lines for cat eyes. Use remaining pearls for mouth. Glue purple rose on as nose.
4. Glue narrow ribbon around cat neck. Use wider ribbon to gather into a circle and glue along side of neck. Glue ribbon roses in a cluster to the center of the ribbon circle.

PEACOCK FEATHER & POD DESIGN

This masculine design is perfect for the den or family room (FIG. 13-4). You will need:

☐ One 10-inch (25.5 cm) wicker mat

☐ One sponge mushroom 12 inches (30.5 cm) across

☐ 2 yards (1.8 m) of 1-inch-wide (2.5 cm) blue gauze-like ribbon

☐ Three blue whitewashed lotus pods, each 3 inches (7.5 cm) wide

☐ Six bleached yanagimaki stems (curly rattan)

☐ Five 2-inch (5 cm) pinecones on stems

☐ Twelve natural peacock feathers

☐ 1/2 block Sahara II floral foam

☐ 1-ounce package Spanish moss

☐ Hot-glue gun and sticks, white craft glue

☐ 1 chenille stem

1. Cut the foam block in half and glue one half to the back of the wicker

Fig. 13-3 (Above Left) The statice used to cover the cat adds a soft romantic feeling to the design.

Fig. 13-4 (Above Right) This peacock feather design adds a masculine touch.

mat. Insert the stem of the sponge mushroom in the front of the foam and glue the other half on top of the sponge mushroom.

2. Cut the stem of one feather to 18 inches (45.5 cm) and insert it into the back center of the foam. Use nine more feathers and insert into the foam, forming the outside triangle shape as shown in FIG. 13-4.

3. Insert the lotus pods with 4-inch (10 cm) stems in a cluster into the center of the design.

4. Form a bow with the ribbon having 4-inch (10 cm) loops, secure with chenille stem, and insert into center of design between pods.

5. Cut stems of remaining feathers shorter and insert around ribbon loops and pods. Cut stems of yanagimaki and pods at various lengths and insert within the triangle shape formed by the peacock feathers.

BASIC WALL BASKET

The basics of this design can be repeated for any style of basket, either for a wall or table. Always begin with the filler materials first, filling and forming the basic shape of the arrangement. Next add the other materials designed to create interest in the design (FIG. 13-5).

You will need:

☐ One 6-inch-tall (15 cm) basket with 6-inch-wide (15 cm) opening

☐ 5-inch (12.5 cm) × 3-inch (7.5 cm) block Sahara II foam

☐ 1-ounce bag sphagnum moss

☐ 2-ounce package preserved galaxy gypsophila

☐ 10 pencil cattails

☐ 24 pieces wheat

☐ 6-ounce bunch orange hill flowers

☐ 36 stems teal lagurus (bunny tails)

☐ 32 wired wood picks

☐ U-shaped craft pins

☐ Hot-glue gun and sticks

1. Glue foam into container, cover with moss, and secure with craft pins.

2. Follow the instructions in chapter 4 for the casual mass design style as a guide for this design. Break the galaxy gyp stems to lengths of 4 inches (10 cm) to 9 inches (22.5 cm). Insert these throughout the basket to create a full, rounded look.

3. Cut the cattail stems to 3 inches (7.5 cm). Insert all pieces into the design, with the center ones being straighter in the design and those to the outside angling into the foam.

4. Cut the wheat stems to 1 inch (2.5 cm). Place three together and attach to a wood pick. Insert these deep into the arrangement. Equally space these picks around the design.

5. Place approximately 12 pieces of hill flowers together of different lengths. Cut all stems to approximately 2-inch (2.5 cm) to 3-inch (7.5 cm) lengths. Attach to a wood pick and insert into the foam. Create a total of 12 bunches and place throughout the design to add color.
6. Repeat step 5 with the lagurus, using three heads per pick.

COUNTRY POTPOURRI BASKET

Peach potpourri filling this basket creates a marvelous aroma as well as wonderful changes in color and texture (FIG. 13-6).

You will need:

☐ One 10-inch-wide (25.5 cm) × 4-inch-tall (10 cm) peach flaired basket
☐ 12 white palm deglets
☐ 1-ounce peach potpourri
☐ 2 yards (1.8 m) of 2-inch-wide (5 cm) peach whitewashed paper ribbon
☐ 1-ounce bundle blue-green Florentine flowers
☐ 1-ounce mauve lagurus (bunny tails)
☐ ½ block Sahara II foam
☐ One chenille stem
☐ Wired wood picks   ☐ U-shaped craft pins
☐ 1-ounce Spanish moss   ☐ Hot-glue gun and sticks

Fig. 13-5 (Above Left)
The wall basket is lovely and can be extremely versatile.

Fig. 13-6 (Above Right)
The whitewashed and pastel colors in this design give the feeling of a more contemporary country styling.

1. Glue foam into container, cover with moss, and secure with pins.
2. Cut three palm deglet stems to 18-inch lengths (45.5 cm) and insert into center back of foam. Cut four stems to 14-inch lengths (35 cm) and insert around 18-inch (45.5 cm) stems. Cut last five to 12-inch lengths (30.5 cm) and insert around grouping.
3. Spread potpourri over moss in basket. Form a four loop bow, with the paper ribbon having 5-inch (12.5 cm) loops and 12-inch (30.5 cm) streamers. Secure with chenille stem, twist ends of chenille together, cut to 4-inch (10 cm) length, and insert into front of foam, glueing streamers to basket edges.
4. Break off pieces of Florentine 3 inches (7.5 cm) to 10 inches (25.5 cm) and insert into a grouping in the right side of the basket.
5. Repeat step 4 for lagurus stems; however, before inserting stems into the left side of the basket, attach 6 to 8 stems to a wood pick.

POTPOURRI BASKET

Decorate the handles and rims of any basket that will fit with the decor of your room and fill the center with fragrant potpourri. (Refer to page 3 of the color section, upper left, for project picture).

You will need:

☐ One 12-inch-tall (30.5 cm) × 10-inch-wide (25.5 cm) flat open basket
☐ 4-ounce bunch bleached glittered galaxy gypsophila
☐ 3 yards (2.5 m) of 1/2-inch-wide (1.3 cm) mauve woven-edge ribbon
☐ 2-ounce bundle purple statice sinuata
☐ 3-ounce bundle pink campo flowers
☐ Potpourri of your choice to fill basket
☐ Six 18-inch lengths of cloth-covered wire
☐ White floral tape
☐ Hot-glue gun and sticks, white craft glue

1. Holding two pieces of cloth-covered wire together, floral-tape two other pieces end-to-end, with the first two overlapping 4 inches (10 cm). Measure wire around top of handle and cut to fit.
2. Form small 2-inch (5 cm) to 3-inch (7.5 cm) bunches of galaxy gyp and floral-tape to the wire. Repeat, placing second bunch under first. Continue to end of wire.
3. Break off 2-inch (5 cm) pieces galaxy gypsophila and glue around the basket rim.
4. Pinch ribbon and secure with 1-inch (2.5 cm) piece cloth-covered wire every 6 inches (15 cm). Glue the pinched portion into gyp, circling rim and handle.
5. Break off statice heads and glue throughout gypsophila. Make small bunches of 6 to 8 campo flowers and glue throughout gypsophila.
6. Fill the basket with potpourri.

Index